GREEN &BLACK'S

CHOCOLATE RECIPES

The mysterious *Theobroma cacao* grows wild in the Amazon River Basin and the foothills of the Venezuelan and Colombian Andes, where it is believed the first cacao trees were found.

GREEN &BLACK'S

CHOCOLATE RECIPES

FROM THE CACAO POD
TO MUFFINS, MOUSSES, AND MOLES

Written and compiled by Caroline Jeremy
Photography by Francesca Yorke
Designed by Claire Fry

KYLE BOOKS

"Chocolate makes otherwise normal people melt into strange states of ecstasy" *John West*

To the Maya cacao farmers
and all those cooks who have shared
their recipes over the years.

CONTENTS

FOREWORD BY JOSEPHINE FAIRLEY

When Green & Black's was launched in 1991, we cheekily declared it to be "guilt-free" chocolate. As the world's very first organic chocolate, it gave passionate chocolate-lovers a way to indulge their tastebuds without having an environmental impact – because conventionally grown cacao is still one of the most heavily sprayed food crops in the world. Because Green & Black's was organic – just beginning, then, to be a buzzword – people were intrigued enough to buy and try it. But we know that what makes someone buy any Green & Black's treat a second time – and a hundredth time – is sheer deliciousness. Quite simply, every new Green & Black's creation has to be the best of its kind that we've ever tasted. End of story.

Gradually, though, in the last decade, most of us have begun to think much more about where our food comes from. And at Green & Black's, we like to think we've helped change the world – one bar of chocolate at a time. Because we weren't just the world's first organic chocolate. In 1993, our orange-and-spice Maya Gold Chocolate became the very first product to carry the Fairtrade Mark – the shopper's guarantee that the farmers and growers who produce our cacao get a fairer price for their crops.

This was a shopping revolution. The day of Maya Gold's launch, Green & Black's had a total of eight minutes' of news coverage on primetime TV. Because Maya Gold's debut coincided with an independent campaign for fair trade, we discovered to our astonishment that thousands of Young Methodists were actually running from town to town carrying flaming torches and button-holing supermarket managers to stock this ground-breaking Fairtrade-marked product. One supermarket buyer complained to us that he'd even been getting phone calls from vicars, badgering him to stock Maya Gold because of its ethical integrity. (Nothing to do with us, though we were secretly thrilled to have that unexpected boost to our sales drive!) But that buyer still placed an order – and today, awareness of fair trade issues means most global coffee-shop empires even offer a Fairtrade-marked *cappuccino* on their menus, while shoppers can fill shopping baskets not only with fairly traded chocolate and cocoa powder, but tea, coffee, bananas, and more.

Actually, we didn't have to do anything very special to get that Fairtrade Mark: it was how we naturally did business. It was only later that we realized that we had established a blueprint for socially responsible business which many big companies are striving towards, today. Green & Black's already paid a higher price than the world price – because we offered a premium for organic beans. We gave the farmers the security of long-term contracts – because we also needed that security, at a time when organic cocoa wasn't traded anywhere on the world markets and we needed to be sure of a reliable supply. Since then, though, we've been able to see the incredible impact that fair trade has on a community.

When we first started buying cacao from the Maya Indians in Belize, children left school at eleven because their parents couldn't pay for their board during the week at the high school in Punta Gorda, or even afford their essential high school books. Now, as a result of the secure income from Green & Black's, a whole generation of children from the hillside villages where our chocolate grows is being educated to the age of eighteen; some are even attending university and at least one plans to study medicine. As Cayetano Ico, the former chairman of the co-operative of cacao farmers who produce the cacao for Maya Gold once said: "when you buy a bar of Green & Black's, you're sending a child to school." Shopping ethically really does change lives and communities for the better. But we've always believed: fairly traded products also have to be as yummy – or yummier – than what else is out there. Otherwise, shoppers wouldn't buy it more than once, and then the lives of Third World farmers and growers wouldn't be transformed, after all.

People often ask how Green & Black's got its name. In fact, it was dreamed up one rainy Saturday night by me and my husband, Whole Earth Foods founder (and now Chairman of the Soil Association), Craig Sams, while searching for a name for the chocolate we planned to launch together. There was never a Mr. Green & a Mr. Black, I'm afraid: just a couple sitting in bed with a notepad and a pen, having terrific fun brainstorming. As a lifelong candy-lover, I remembered confectionery brands from my childhood, that had stayed in my mind: Callard & Bowser, Barker & Dobson. And so Green (because it was organic) & Black's (because the chocolate was such a dark brown, it was almost black) was born. If we'd stuck to some of the names we originally batted back and forth – like "Eco-Choc" or "Bio-Choc" – that very same dark chocolate would simply have gathered dust on the shelves, and very few people would have discovered its tastebud-caressing deliciousness. And somehow I don't feel I'd be writing the introduction to a cookbook devoted to it.

Our other important "first," meanwhile, was that Green & Black's was the first chocolate with 70% cocoa content available in the UK. In continental Europe, chocolate *aficionados* have long enjoyed the rich, bitter intensity of really dark chocolate. But in England, the "dark" chocolate we all grew up with actually contained as little as 30% cocoa. But since Green & Black's was launched, 70% dark chocolate has become the magic figure quoted by cookbook writers and superchefs whenever they publish a recipe that uses chocolate: quite simply, for the ultimate in chocolatiness, there's nothing better.

In the early days at Green & Black's, we printed a small recipe leaflet that featured recipes from leading chefs (at Launceston Place and The Groucho Club), alongside temptations from our (much-missed) friend Linda McCartney and others who'd generously shared their outrageous chocolate creations with us. We always dreamed, one day, of a Green & Black's cookbook, featuring the ultimate chocolate recipes – and here it is. Caroline Jeremy has done a marvelous job of writing this book, and collating (and testing) the many recipes sent to us over the years, by Green & Black's lovers, and also of persuading other leading cooks and chefs who are fans to reveal to us (and to you) their chocolate recipe secrets.

We hope you enjoy making, eating, and sharing them. Entirely guilt-free, naturally.

Josephine Fairley

INTRODUCTION

Christened *Theobroma* which means "food of the gods," cocoa is indisputably one of the most desired and valuable substances in the world. Purists would say that it is at its best used in a bar of chocolate, unadulterated by any other taste. But we think it can be just as exciting when transformed into a dessert or cake, or more unexpectedly, into a hearty stew or spicy sausage.

It is not an easy ingredient to create something new with, or something different, but we have searched through our treasured library of recipes, collected over our thirteen years in chocolate, and have chosen the best of them for this book.

Chocolate can surprise even the greatest of chefs, but it is not difficult or frightening to use. Be patient and gentle and take your time. Above all, chocolate should not be hurried.

Any recipe in this book made with good-quality chocolate will taste dramatically different if made with an inferior chocolate, so choose your chocolate carefully. For most of the recipes, we have used our Dark Chocolate, which has 70% cocoa content and very little sugar. It is generally the best chocolate to use for cooking because its intense flavor is not easily overpowered by competing flavors or other ingredients. Avoid dark chocolates that have less than 60% cocoa content and are not made with natural vanilla. Vanillin, which is an artificial flavoring, and vegetable fat, gives the chocolate a very different flavor and texture from chocolate that contains natural vanilla and cocoa butter.

Where milk chocolate is specified, try to use milk chocolate that has at least 34% cocoa content. White chocolate only contains cocoa butter from the cacao bean, not the dark solids. If white chocolate does not declare a percentage of cocoa content, it will not contain cocoa butter. It will probably also not have natural vanilla in it, which gives our chocolate its unique flavour.

An unsweetened cocoa powder is best for baking.

COOKING WITH CHOCOLATE

• Always store chocolate in a cool, dry place and do not expose to direct light. Chocolate that has been exposed to extremes in temperature or light will "bloom," or have whitish-gray streaks on it. These streaks indicate that the cocoa butter in the chocolate has changed its structure and crystallized on the surface. This does not affect the flavor though, and once melted, the chocolate will be fine to use for cooking.

• Never store chocolate near other household items or foods that have a strong scent. Chocolate absorbs odors easily and will soon taste of other flavors if stored near them. This is especially true of mint, citrus fruit, perfumes, and chemicals, so be careful when packing your shopping.

Chocoholic, n. 1. Someone whose constant craving for and delight in chocolate suggests addiction. 2. A person who eats chocolate compulsively.

• To melt chocolate, break or chop it up into even-sized pieces using your hands or a large sharp knife. Place it in the top of a double boiler or else in a dry, heatproof bowl and sit it over a saucepan of barely simmering water. Never allow steam or water to come into direct contact with the chocolate, and make sure the bottom of the top pan or the bowl is not touching the water. This is especially important if you are melting white chocolate, which is particularly sensitive to over-heating. After two minutes, turn off the heat and leave the bowl over the saucepan of hot water while the chocolate slowly melts. Stir gently as soon as most of the chocolate has melted, and remove the bowl from the heat.

• Chocolate can also be easily melted in a bowl in a microwave oven. Cook on medium for one minute, then, depending on the quantity, in 30-second bursts. Keep checking the chocolate by prodding it with a spoon as it will keep its shape despite it having melted.

• Chocolate that has been overheated may "seize" or become very thick and lumpy and impossible to use. If this does happen, you can try whisking in a pat of butter or a little vegetable oil, but you may not be able to save it if it has gone too far.

• Try to have melted chocolate at a similar temperature to the mixture you are adding it to.

• Never try to melt chocolate by adding a hot mixture to solid chocolate or vice versa, unless the recipe specifically instructs you to. The result will be grainy in texture.

• Melting chocolate with liquids is fine if specified but start melting all the required ingredients together — never add any once the chocolate has begun to melt as this may cause it to seize.

• If you need to grate chocolate, place the bar in the fridge overnight before grating and make sure your hands are cold.

• Tempering chocolate, which we describe in detail on page 150, is only necessary if you are dipping or coating for an extremely important occasion and want to guarantee a brittle snap and gloss. Tempering is a complicated procedure, but as bars of chocolate are already tempered when you buy them, you could try this simpler version instead.

SIMPLE TEMPERING

The stable fat crystals do not melt until 94°F so, in theory, if the chocolate is never heated above 91–92°F, the temper won't be lost. The trick is to barely melt the chocolate. Into a bowl, grate the chocolate finely so it will melt quickly and evenly. Heat a thick-bottomed saucepan of water until it boils and then remove from the heat. Place the bowl of chocolate over the saucepan and stir gently, but constantly, until the chocolate has melted. For dark chocolate, the temperature should end up between 89–91°F and between 87–89°F for milk and white. It is then ready to use.

Caroline Jeremy

July 2003

MAGIC

The magical ingredient in chocolate comes from a pod
that grows out of the trunk of a tree.

This very beautiful variation on clafoutis, a French batter and fruit dessert, is two recipes in one. The red wine jello is a special surprise that can be served with the deep red pear clafoutis, or alone as a fun end to a light meal.

CLAFOUTIS WITH CHOCOLATE
AND PEARS IN RED WINE

Preparation time: 25 minutes
Cooking time: 30 minutes
Chilling time: Poach the pears about 6 hours in advance
if you plan to eat the clafoutis hot with the pear and red wine jello
Use: 2 x tarte Tatin or quiche dishes about 9 inches diameter and 1$\frac{1}{2}$ inches deep
Serves: 8

6 pears, just ripe

750ml bottle red wine

juice of 1 lemon

1 cup superfine sugar

2 leaves gelatin
(if unavailable, use $\frac{1}{2}$-package granulated gelatin

one 3$\frac{1}{2}$-oz. bar dark chocolate,
minimum 60% cocoa content, broken into pieces

$\frac{1}{3}$ cup ($\frac{3}{4}$ stick) unsalted butter

1 cup self-rising flour

1 cup ground almonds

pinch of salt

2 large eggs

1 large egg yolk

$\frac{3}{4}$ cup whole milk

Crème fraîche or sour cream, for serving

Peel the pears, but leave the stalks on, then place them in a saucepan, along with the red wine, lemon juice, and half of the sugar. Bring slowly to a boil, then reduce the heat to a gentle simmer and poach the pears for about 10 minutes. Turn off the heat, turn the pears in the poaching liquid, then leave them in the liquid to cool for about two hours.

Reserve the liquid to make the jello. Slice the pears in half and remove the cores carefully with a knife.

To make the jello, reheat the poaching liquid until hot but not simmering, remove from the heat, and add the gelatin. Stir, and pour into a bowl to chill for four hours.

Preheat the oven to 400°F.

Melt the chocolate in the top of a double boiler over barely simmering water.

Melt the butter and brush some of it over the inside of the baking dishes. Set aside the remainder.

Sift the flour into a bowl and then add the ground almonds, the remaining sugar, and the salt. Whisk together the eggs, egg yolk, and milk, and add to the dry ingredients, whisking until smooth. Add the melted chocolate and remaining butter and stir until fully incorporated.

Divide the mixture between the two baking dishes, then place the pear halves, with the thinner end facing inwards, around the dish, with some of the pears face up and some face down.

Bake for 20 minutes. A skewer inserted in the clafoutis will not come out clean; it is important that it remains slightly gooey.

Serve hot or cold, with crème fraîche and the red wine and pear jello.

HINT: A melon baller is perfect for removing the core from a pear.

MAGIC

Launceston Place is a calm and friendly restaurant tucked away in Kensington, London. They gave us this recipe in the early 1990s, when they first discovered Green & Black's chocolate.

CHOCOLATE

BERRY TORTE

Preparation time: 25 minutes
Cooking time: 40 minutes
Use: a cake pan, 7¹/₂–8 inches across, 2¹/₂ inches deep
Serves: 6

TORTE

¹/₄ cup all-purpose flour

5 teaspoons cocoa powder

3 ounces dark chocolate,
minimum 60% cocoa content broken into pieces

2 tablespoons unsalted butter

5 teaspoons heavy cream

4 egg whites

3 egg yolks

3 tablespoons sugar

9 ounces fresh blueberries or raspberries
(about 1¹/₂–2 cups)

¹/₂ cup whipping cream or heavy cream, for serving

ICING

one 3¹/₂-oz. bar dark chocolate,
minimum 60% cocoa content, broken into pieces

¹/₄ cup (¹/₂ stick) unsalted butter

3 tablespoons heavy cream

1 teaspoon confectioners' sugar

Preheat the oven to 275°F. Butter the cake pan and dust with flour to coat.

Sift together the flour and cocoa and set aside.

Melt the chocolate in the top of a double boiler over barely simmering water. Remove from the heat, add the butter and the cream, and stir well until the mixture is quite liquid.

Beat the egg whites until stiff peaks form, add the sugar, and continue to beat until thick and glossy. In another large bowl, beat together the egg yolks and then gently fold in the flour and cocoa mixture. Add the melted chocolate and mix well. Spoon a few dollops of egg white into the mixture, stir, then gently fold in the remainder of the egg whites.

Gently pour half the mixture into the prepared cake pan, dot half the berries evenly over it, then pour the rest of the mixture on top of the berries.

Bake for 35 to 40 minutes, until a skewer inserted into the center of the cake comes out clean. Cool in the pan for five minutes and unmold onto a wire rack to cool.

To make the icing, melt the chocolate in a heatproof bowl sitting over a saucepan of barely simmering water. Remove from the heat, stir in the butter, cream, and confectioners' sugar. Immediately pour it over the cake to coat it completely, smoothing the icing using a butter knife. Leave for one hour to harden.

Serve with whipped cream and the remaining berries.

HINT: Do not refrigerate this cake once you have iced it
as the icing will lose its shine and become dull and lifeless.

Gerard Coleman and Anne Weyns are the founders of L'Artisan du Chocolat, the most elegant chocolate shop in London. This recipe, which adds coarse salt to the caramel, reflects their expertise in searching for and identifying unusual flavors that enhance good-quality chocolate.

CHOCOLATE AND SALTED CARAMEL

TART

Preparation time: 1 hour
Cooking time: 25 minutes
Use: 11-inch removable-bottomed tart pan
Serves 12–14

PASTRY DOUGH

2¹/₂ cups all-purpose flour

²/₃ cup confectioners' sugar

¹/₂ cup (1 stick) plus 1 tablespoon unsalted butter, cold

2 eggs

CARAMEL

3 tablespoons corn syrup

1¹/₃ cups sugar

²/₃ cup heavy cream

1 level teaspoon coarse salt, such as kosher salt

2 tablespoons unsalted butter, diced

GANACHE

1³/₄ cups heavy cream

3 tablespoons honey

12 ounces dark chocolate, minimum 60% cocoa content, chopped

³/₄ cup (1¹/₂ sticks) unsalted butter, diced

To make the pastry dough, sift together the flour and confectioners' sugar and cut the butter into chunks. Place in the food processor and run it, adding in the eggs at the end, until a dough forms. Roll out the dough using quite a lot of flour as it can stick easily. Place it carefully into the tart pan. Chill in the fridge for about 30 minutes. Preheat the oven to 350°F.

Bake the pie shell blind by covering it with foil or parchment paper, filling with dried beans, and cooking for about 15 to 20 minutes. Remove the beans and paper and continue to cook the pie shell for another 10 minutes or until it has developed a light golden color. Remove and let cool.

To make the caramel, pour the syrup into a deep saucepan and bring to a boil. Add the sugar, gradually stir and continue to cook until the sugar has started to caramelize and has turned a golden brown color. At the same time, in a separate saucepan, bring the cream and salt to a boil. Remove the caramel from the heat and very carefully add the cream to the caramel, but be extremely careful as the mixture will rise rapidly in the saucepan and could cause serious burns. Using an immersion blender, mix until smooth over a low heat. Remove from the heat, add the diced butter, and stir before pouring into the cooled pie shell.

To make the ganache, bring the cream and honey to a boil and pour it over the chopped chocolate. Mix carefully with a spatula, working from the center outwards. Once the mixture has cooled a little, add the diced butter, and stir gently until the butter has melted. Pour the ganache on top of the caramel and let it set in a cool place for about four to six hours.

HINT: This sweet pastry dough shrinks a lot, so when you place the dough in the pan, make sure it reaches high up the sides of the pan.

Our English "biscuit" and Italian "*biscotti*" are both words that derive from the Latin "*biscoctus*" meaning "twice-cooked." Large glass jars of biscotti often grace the counters of Italian coffee shops and usually the biscotti have almonds or hazelnuts in them. They should always be cut at an angle, shaped like a half-moon, and are the perfect partner for a liqueur or a fruity dessert.

MAYA-DUNKED

BISCOTTI

Preparation time: 20 minutes
Cooking time: 45 minutes
Makes: 12

1 ¹/₂ cups all-purpose flour

²/₃ cup cocoa powder

³/₄ teaspoon baking powder

pinch of salt

1 cup sugar

³/₄ tablespoon ground espresso coffee

2 ¹/₂ ounces dark chocolate,
minimum 60% cocoa content, chopped

2 medium eggs

1 medium egg yolk

³/₄ teaspoon vanilla extract

two 3¹/₂–oz. bars Maya Gold chocolate, or other good-quality orange-flavored dark chocolate, broken into pieces

Preheat the oven to 350°F. Cover a baking tray with parchment paper.

Sift together the flour, cocoa, baking powder, salt, and sugar, and place into the food processor. Add the ground coffee and the dark chocolate. Using the pulse button, pulse until finely ground. In a bowl, whisk together the eggs and yolk, add the vanilla extract, and pour into the food processor, running it until the mixture forms a ball.

Lightly flour the counter top and roll the dough into a log. Flour the surface of the log ensuring it is coated on all sides. Place it on the baking tray. Bake the log for 25 to 30 minutes, then remove from the oven and reduce the temperature to 300°F.

Remove the parchment paper with the log on it from the baking tray and let cool. Use a sharp knife to cut across the log at an angle to make slices about a half-inch thick. Place the slices on the baking tray and bake for about 30 minutes, until firm. Let cool.

Melt the chocolate in the top of a double boiler over barely simmering water. Dip one end of each biscotti into the chocolate, and place on a wire rack to set.

HINT: You can use any of your favorite types of chocolate to coat the biscotti.

A hybrid of two of our favorite recipes, this mousse looks beautiful and tastes heavenly, but it does take hours to make, however, and produces piles of dirty dishes, so be prepared. Not for the faint-hearted!

WHITE & DARK CHOCOLATE MOUSSE
WITH RED BERRY COULIS

Preparation time: 20 minutes for each mousse
Chilling time: 2 hours for the dark mousse and then overnight for the white and dark mousse
Use: 7-inch bottomless ring mold
Serves: 8–10

DARK CHOCOLATE MOUSSE

one 3$\frac{1}{2}$-oz. bar dark chocolate, minimum 60% cocoa content, broken into pieces

$\frac{1}{3}$ cup confectioners' sugar

$\frac{1}{3}$ cup ($\frac{3}{4}$ stick) unsalted butter, softened

3 large eggs, separated

scant $\frac{1}{2}$ cup cocoa powder

pinch of salt

$\frac{1}{2}$ cup whipping cream

WHITE CHOCOLATE MOUSSE

two 3$\frac{1}{2}$-oz. bars good-quality white chocolate, broken into pieces

2 leaves gelatin or $\frac{1}{2}$-package granulated gelatin

1$\frac{1}{4}$ cups whipping cream

3 large egg yolks

1 cup confectioners' sugar

2 tablespoons water

2 tablespoons Grand Marnier

RED BERRY COULIS

8 ounces strawberries or raspberries

$\frac{1}{3}$ cup confectioners' sugar

FOR DECORATING

$\frac{1}{4}$ cup of cocoa powder or

2 cartons of fresh raspberries

To make the dark chocolate mousse, melt the chocolate in the top of a double boiler over barely simmering water. Add the confectioners' sugar and stir in the butter, then beat in the egg yolks and the cocoa and salt.

In a bowl, whisk the egg whites until stiff peaks start to form. In another bowl, whip the cream until thick, then gently fold the egg whites and the cream alternately into the chocolate mixture. Do not overmix, but ensure that the mixture is well blended.

Place the ring mold on a large, round serving plate. Pour the mousse into the mold and chill for about two hours before making the white chocolate mousse.

To make the white chocolate mousse, melt the white chocolate in the top of a double boiler over barely simmering water. Ensure that the water does not touch the bottom of the top pan as white chocolate is especially sensitive to overheating. Dissolve the gelatin in about a quarter-cup of cream that has been warmed in a saucepan.

Whisk the egg yolks and confectioners' sugar until thick and creamy and then add the Grand Marnier, the gelatin and cream mixture, and the melted chocolate.

HINT: This mousse should be refrigerated before serving, especially on a hot day, but don't add the cocoa powder and coulis until you are ready to serve.

Whip the remainder of the cream until thick, and fold it into the white chocolate mixture.

Pour the white mousse on top of the dark mousse that has already set, and chill overnight.

To make the coulis, purée the berries in a blender and then strain through a fine strainer into a bowl. Stir in the confectioners' sugar to taste.

To unmold the mousse, dip a butter knife or pastry spatula in boiling water, dry it, then slide it around the inside edge of the mold. Lift the ring mold off carefully and smooth the sides of the mousse with the knife.

To serve, sift the cocoa over the top of the mousse to cover, or scatter with whole raspberries. Pour some of the coulis onto the plate around the edge of the mousse and serve the remainder from a pitcher. Slice the mousse using a pastry spatula dipped in hot water.

Micah Carr-Hill has the coveted job of chocolate taster at Green & Black's and is the creative genius behind our products. He also loves to educate those around him in the art of eating and often arrives at work with anything from stuffed ox cheeks to Portuguese custard tarts. These ice cream balls are a variation on a recipe he created for one of our ice cream promotions.

DEEP-FRIED CHOCOLATE NUT
ICE CREAM BALLS

Preparation time: 30 minutes
Freezing time: 30 minutes
Frying time: 90 seconds per 3 balls
Use: Ice cream scoop, non-stick baking tray that fits in the freezer, a deep-fat fryer or deep saucepan
Makes: 10

1 pint (16 fl. oz.) tub good-quality dark chocolate ice cream

1 pack of phyllo dough sheets

1 large egg yolk

$1/2$ cup milk

1–2 quarts sunflower or canola oil for deep-frying

1 teaspoon confectioners' sugar

1 cup hazelnuts, chopped and toasted

2 ounces dark chocolate, minimum 60% cocoa content grated, for sprinkling

Take a tub of dark chocolate ice cream out of the freezer and let it soften for 10 minutes. Scoop into balls using an ice cream scoop dipped in hot water, place them on a non-stick baking tray, and return to the freezer for half an hour to harden.

Meanwhile prepare the pastry dough. Cut the phyllo dough sheets into five-inch squares (you will need 30). Make an egg wash by whisking together the egg yolk, milk, and confectioners' sugar. Take a square of phyllo dough, brush it with egg wash and sprinkle the hazelnuts over it. Lay a second square over the first at an angle and repeat the brushing and sprinkling. Repeat the process with a final square. Continue until you have ten, triple layers of phyllo squares brushed with egg wash, and sprinkled with nuts.

Preheat a heavy saucepan (or a deep-fat fryer), one-third filled with oil, to 350°F.

Take the ice cream balls out of the freezer and place one in the center of each triple layer of phyllo squares. Carefully wrap the phyllo around the balls without tearing the dough. If you are not deep-frying the balls right away, put them back in the freezer until you need them so that the ice cream does not melt.

Using a metal slotted spoon, put the ice cream balls into the hot oil (no more than three at a time to ensure the oil does not cool down too much) and fry until golden brown; this will take about 90 seconds. Remove and drain on paper towels. Serve immediately with shavings of dark chocolate.

HINT: Buy a deep-frying thermometer (they are not expensive) to ensure the temperature of the oil is hot enough. If the oil cools down it will soak into the dough and melt the ice cream rather than creating a crisp pastry with insulating air pockets.

Only make this cake for celebrations. It was created the night before a photographic shoot when we realized the front cover of a recipe leaflet we had designed needed a photograph of a taller cake. The bottom layer is our "Dark Chocolate Mousse Cake" and the top is the "Taillevent Terrine" recipe picked up in the Eighties from the great Parisian restaurant that bears the name.

MARQUISE
AU CHOCOLAT

Preparation time: 50 minutes
Cooking time: 40 minutes
Cooling time: 2 hours
Chilling time: overnight
Use: 9-inch springform pan with high sides and removable bottom
Makes: 15 small, rich, slices

CAKE LAYER

melted butter for greasing

1 tablespoon ground almonds,
plus extra for dusting the pan

three 3^1/$_2$-oz. bars dark chocolate, minimum 60% cocoa content (or two 3^1/$_2$-oz. bars dark chocolate, minimum 60% cocoa content, and one 3^1/$_2$-oz. bar Maya Gold or good-quality dark orange-flavored chocolate), broken into pieces

1^1/$_4$ cups sugar

^{2}/$_3$ cup (1^1/$_4$ sticks) plus 1 tablespoon unsalted butter

pinch sea salt or kosher salt

5 large eggs

MOUSSE

9 ounces dark chocolate,
minimum 60% cocoa content, broken into pieces

^{3}/$_4$ cup confectioners' sugar

^{3}/$_4$ cup (1^1/$_2$ sticks) unsalted butter

5 large eggs, separated

^{2}/$_3$ cup whipping cream

cocoa powder for dusting

Preheat the oven to 350°F.

Brush the pan with melted butter and dust with the ground almonds, shaking off any excess.

To make the cake, melt the chocolate, sugar, butter, and salt in a large, heatproof bowl over a saucepan of barely simmering water, then remove from the heat.

Whisk the eggs with the ground almonds and fold into the chocolate mixture. Continue to fold until the mixture thickens. Pour into the cake pan and bake for 35 to 40 minutes. Let cool in the pan for about two hours before starting the mousse.

To make the mousse, melt the chocolate in a large, heatproof bowl sitting over a saucepan of barely simmering water. Remove from the heat and add half the confectioners' sugar, stir, then whisk in the butter. Whisk in the egg yolks, one at a time. Set the mixture aside.

Whisk the egg whites until stiff peaks start to form. Add the remaining confectioners' sugar and continue to whisk until glossy. Whip the cream until stiff peaks form.

Add one-third of the egg whites in a large bowl to the chocolate mixture and carefully mix to blend. Gently fold in the remaining whites, alternating with the whipped cream. Do not overmix, but ensure that the mixture is well blended. Pour the mousse over the cooled cake in the cake pan and refrigerate overnight.

Remove the pan from the refrigerator about 15 minutes before serving. Dip a butter knife into boiling water, dry it, and slide it around the sides of the cake to loosen it from the pan, then remove the ring. Reheat the butter knife in boiling water, dry it, and gently smooth the sides of the mousse.

Place the cake, still on the pan's bottom, onto a large round serving plate. Dust generously with cocoa powder just before serving. Serve with crème fraîche or a custard sauce (see page 61).

MAGIC

You must have had people ask you whether you have tried Nigella Lawson's Clementine Cake? It is one of those recipes that fans of Nigella always mention and is so incredibly easy to make, it never fails. It is also the perfect partner for some melted Maya Gold Chocolate, especially at Christmas time when clementines are at their best.

NIGELLA'S

CLEMENTINE CAKE

Preparation time: 15 minutes
Cooking time: 2 hours to cook the clementines, 1 hour to bake the cake
Use: 8-inch springform cake pan

4–5 clementines, skin on, weighing about 13 ounces

melted butter for greasing

6 large eggs

1 cup sugar

2³/₄ cups ground almonds

1 heaped teaspoon baking powder

one 3¹/₂-oz. bar Maya Gold Chocolate, or other good-quality, dark, orange-flavored chocolate

Put the clementines into a saucepan, cover with cold water, bring to a boil and simmer for about two hours. Drain and set aside to cool. Then cut each clementine in half and remove the seeds. Then pulp everything – skins, pith, and the fruit in a food processor.

Preheat the oven to 375°F. Butter the cake pan, dust with ground almonds, and shake out any excess.

Beat the eggs. Add the sugar, almonds, and baking powder. Mix well, add the pulped clementines, then stir together. Pour the mixture into the cake pan and bake for one hour or until a skewer inserted into the center of the cake comes out clean. Cover the cake with foil after about 40 minutes to prevent the top from burning. Remove from the oven and immediately grate the chocolate over the top of the cake while still in the pan. Let it cool completely. Remove from the pan and store in an airtight container.

HINT: Don't be tempted to serve this cake warm. It must only be eaten once it has cooled as the texture becomes moist and the flavours of the almonds and oranges have taken hold. It is best served the day after it is made.

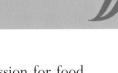

Paul and Jeanne Rankin met while they were both traveling the world. Their passion for food grew while working in restaurant kitchens when funds ran out, and after training at Albert Roux's La Gavroche, they opened Roscoff in Belfast, which went on to win a Michelin star. Their latest restaurant, Cayenne, specializes in food with a hint of spice.

WHITE CHOCOLATE AND HAZELNUT CHEESECAKE
WITH ORANGE CARAMEL SAUCE

Preparation time: 1 hour
Cooking time: 1½ hours
Cooling time: at least 3 hours or overnight
Use: 9-inch springform pan
Serves: 10–12

CRUST

1½ cups crumbled vanilla wafers

1 tablespoon sugar

3 tablespoons unsalted butter, melted

FILLING

³/₄ cup hazelnuts

¹/₃ cup sugar

2¹/₄ pounds cream cheese

4 large eggs

1 large egg yolk

1 vanilla bean, split lengthwise, or 1 teaspoon vanilla extract

1 tablespoon Amaretto

pinch of freshly grated nutmeg

11 ounces good-quality white chocolate, broken into pieces (about 2 cups)

confectioners' sugar for dusting

ORANGE CARAMEL SAUCE

2¹/₄ cups orange juice

3 tablespoons sugar

1¹/₂ teaspoons arrowroot

2 tablespoons Grand Marnier

Preheat the oven to 400°F.

To make the crust, grind the cookies to a fine texture in a blender or food processor. In a bowl, combine the crushed cookies with the sugar and melted butter. Press the mixture onto the bottom of the springform pan.

To make the filling, roast the hazelnuts on a dry baking tray in the oven for 10 to 15 minutes until golden, then rub off their skins. Reduce the temperature to 300°F. Put the sugar, along with two tablespoons water in a pan and heat gently to dissolve, then boil until it is a rich caramel color. Place the hazelnuts on an oiled tray and pour the caramel syrup on top. Let harden, then break into pieces and pulse in a food processor until coarsely ground. Set aside.

Pulse the cream cheese in a food processor until smooth, then work in the eggs and egg yolk, the seeds scraped from the vanilla bean (or the vanilla extract), Amaretto, and nutmeg. Blend until smooth. Melt the white chocolate in the top of a double boiler over barely simmering water, ensuring that the water does not touch the bottom of the top pan. Add the melted chocolate to the mixture and, finally, the ground hazelnuts. Pour the mixture over the crust and bake for about one and a half hours until lightly set. Switch off the oven and let it go cold and set. Remove from the oven and dust with confectioners' sugar.

To make the Orange Caramel Sauce, put the orange juice in a saucepan and boil rapidly to reduce it by one third. Put the sugar with one tablespoon water in a pan and heat gently to dissolve, then bring to a boil and boil until it is a rich caramel color. Reduce the heat, pour the juice into the sugar pan and simmer until dissolved. Blend the arrowroot with a little water to make a smooth paste, then stir into the orange caramel until the mixture has thickened. Strain through a wire mesh strainer and stir in the liqueur. Let it cool.

To serve, pour some sauce onto individual plates and place a slice of cake in the center.

My daughter, Chloë, is 6 years old and loves to dig into a wobbly soufflé. She also loves to eat her grandfather's specialty, perfectly ripe, sliced mangoes marinated in orange juice. This recipe with its chocolate edges is the one she asks for on special occasions.

MANGO, ORANGE, AND LEMON
SOUFFLÉS

Preparation time: 1 hour, 20 minutes
Cooking time: 10 minutes
Use: 8 ramekins or custard cups
Serves: 8

9 ounces canned mango slices (about 1 heaped cup, and their juice)

4^1/$_2$ ounces dried mangoes (about ^{3}/$_4$ cup)

^{1}/$_3$ cup freshly squeezed orange juice

finely grated rind of 2 lemons

3 tablespoons melted butter for brushing ramekins

5 ounces dark chocolate, minimum 60% cocoa content, finely grated (about 1^1/$_2$–2 cups)

1 cup whole milk

5 tablespoons unsalted butter

3 tablespoons flour

6 large eggs, separated

^{1}/$_2$ cup sugar

Strain the mangoes, draining the juice into a saucepan. Add the dried mangoes to the juice in the saucepan. Bring to simmering point and cook until the mangoes are tender and most of the liquid has been absorbed.

Put the contents of the saucepan, the reserved canned mangoes, and the orange juice into a blender or food processor and whizz to a smooth purée. Stir in the lemon rind and let cool to room temperature.

Preheat the oven to 400°F.

Brush the insides of the ramekins with the melted butter, then sprinkle on the grated chocolate, turning the dishes to ensure all the sides are evenly coated with a thick covering of chocolate. Tap out any excess and set it aside for sprinkling over the finished soufflés. Place the ramekins on a baking tray to make it easier to remove them from the oven.

Heat the milk in a small saucepan. In a large saucepan melt the butter, then remove from the heat and stir in the flour. Return to a low heat and cook, stirring for a few minutes. When the roux starts to foam, gradually whisk in the milk. Cook over medium heat for a few minutes more, until thickened. Remove from the heat and let cool before whisking in the egg yolks, one at a time. Let cool completely and then stir in the mango and orange purée.

Whisk the egg whites until soft peaks form. Gradually whisk in the sugar and continue to whisk until the meringue is firm. Stir a generous spoonful of meringue into the mango mixture to lighten it, then gently fold the mango mixture into the remaining meringue.

Fill the ramekins and bake for 8 to 10 minutes. Do not overfill the soufflés or they will tip over and collapse. Also, remember never to open the oven door; if you don't have a light in your oven, peep at them but try not to let too much air into the oven. The soufflés will rise dramatically.

Carefully remove the soufflés from the oven and sprinkle the reserved grated chocolate over the top. Using a spatula, lift the dishes onto small dessert plates and serve at once before they collapse.

TIME TO SHINE

The Toledo Cocoa Growers Association (T.C.G.A.) is a cooperative of 172 subsistence farmers. Most are Maya people, who grow cacao for us in Belize. The fairtrade contract and the premium price they can command for their organic cacao ensure that they have a stable economic future.

Don't be afraid: like so many of the pastry chef's techniques, this cake is incredibly easy once you know how, and always looks spectacularly impressive even if your piping goes a bit wobbly. The French call it a *"damier"* which means "checkerboard." This is a tall, three-layered cake and when cut, each slice is a checkerboard of chocolate and vanilla.

CHECKERBOARD

Preparation time: 20 minutes
Cooking time: 20 minutes
Use: three 8 x 8-inch cake pans, 2 x pastry bags with ¹/₂-inch plain or fluted nozzles.
Serves: 8–10

VANILLA BATTER

1 cup (2 sticks) unsalted butter

1 cup sugar

4 large eggs

1 teaspoon vanilla extract

2 cups all-purpose flour

1 tablespoon baking powder

CHOCOLATE BATTER

1 cup (2 sticks) unsalted butter

1 cup sugar

4 large eggs

1²/₃ cups all-purpose flour

¹/₂ cup cocoa powder

1 tablespoon baking powder

SUGAR SYRUP

1¹/₄ cups sugar

1¹/₄ cups water

1 tablespoon rum

2 tablespoons apricot jam

GANACHE

5 ounces dark chocolate,
minimum 60% cocoa content, broken into pieces

²/₃ cup whipping cream

Preheat the oven to 375°F.

Butter the cake pans, line the bottoms with circles of waxed paper, then butter the paper.

Begin by making the sugar syrup. Put the sugar and water in a saucepan and bring to a boil, without stirring, and boil until it begins to thicken. Remove from the heat and add the rum. Set aside.

To make the vanilla batter, cream together the butter and sugar thoroughly.

Add the eggs, one by one, mixing well between each addition, then add the vanilla extract.

Sift together the flour and baking powder and add to the mixture, stirring well. The mixture will be quite stiff. Set aside while you make the second batch.

To make the chocolate batter, cream together the butter and the caster sugar thoroughly. Add the eggs, one by one, mixing well between each addition.

Sift together the flour, cocoa, and the baking powder, and add to the mixture, stirring well. The mixture will be quite stiff.

Place the decorating nozzles securely in the pastry bags. Put all the vanilla mixture into one of the bags, and the chocolate mixture into the other. Place the three prepared baking pans in a row.

Starting with the vanilla batter, pipe a ring of vanilla batter inside the outer rim of one of the cake pans.

HINT: This cake becomes even more indulgent if you chop up a bar of our Almond Milk Chocolate into tiny pieces and sprinkle it over the top.

Then pipe a ring of chocolate batter inside the vanilla ring. Continue to pipe alternating rings of vanilla and chocolate batter. There should be six rings of alternating batter, the center one being chocolate. Fill the second cake pan in the same way.

Fill the third cake pan, starting with a chocolate ring and ending with a vanilla ring.

Tap the bottom of each of the cake pans gently on a flat surface to release any air pockets before placing in the oven. Bake for about 20 minutes.

Remove the cakes from the oven, leave in their pans for five minutes to cool slightly. Turn them out onto a wire cooling rack and brush the sugar syrup over the bottom of each cake. Let cool.

Melt the chocolate in the top of a double boiler over barely simmering water. Set aside.

Whip the cream until soft peaks form, then pour the hot chocolate over it in a steady stream, continuing to whip the cream, until the chocolate is just blended.

Once cool, place one of the cakes with a vanilla outer ring on a serving plate, spread apricot jam over the cake, and then top with the cake that has the chocolate outer ring. Spread apricot jam over the second cake, then place the third cake on top.

Using a butter knife or pastry spatula, spread the ganache over the top and sides of the cake to cover it completely.

Amanda Allen has always enjoyed trying recipes from historical cookbooks and has found some intriguing combinations in medieval cooking. She adapted this recipe from Valentina Harris's book, *Regional Italian Cookery*. If you like a strong gamey flavor, you will love this dish, which was invented for the wedding of Caterina de Medici in the early sixteenth century and is typical of the flavors of the time.

TUSCAN SWEET AND SOUR

HARE

Preparation time: 30 minutes
Cooking time: 2 hours
Serves: 4–6

1 large hare

5 cloves garlic

2 sprigs rosemary

5 tablespoons extra virgin olive oil

2 onions, chopped

2 carrots, chopped

1 fennel bulb, chopped

handful parsley

handful basil

3 bay leaves

6 sage leaves

1¼ cups Chianti

2½ cups game stock

1 cup pine nuts

¼ cup golden raisins

⅓ cup candied peel

1 tablespoon granulated sugar

3 cavalluci or almond cookies, ground

2 ounces dark chocolate, minimum 60% cocoa content, broken into chunks

3 tablespoons red wine vinegar

Cut the hare into pieces. Peel and crush the garlic. Briefly fry the hare along with half the garlic, the rosemary, and two tablespoons of oil in a large heavy pan. Remove from the pan with a slotted spoon, discard the garlic and rosemary, and set the hare aside.

In another pan which has a heavy cover, heat the remaining oil and fry the onions, carrots, fennel, herbs, and the rest of the garlic for 10 minutes.

Add the hare to the vegetables and herbs, brown on all sides, then add the wine and heat for a few minutes. Add the game stock, then cover and cook over low heat for one hour and 30 minutes.

In another saucepan, mix together the pine nuts. raisins, peel, sugar, cavalluci, chocolate, and a half-cup water. Heat for 10 minutes over low heat, then remove from the heat and add the vinegar. Pour into the hare stew, stir, then cook for another 10 minutes.

HINT: This dish is best if left to cool overnight and then reheated the next day, as this gives the rich flavors time to infuse and develop.

Chocolate Eruptions was one of the Groucho Club's signature dishes when they first gave it to us many years ago. The Groucho Club is a members-only restaurant and bar in London's West End and it is a favorite with the media, artists, and writers.

CHOCOLATE
ERUPTIONS

Freezing time: 9 hours
Preparation time: 1 hour
Cooking time: 25–30 minutes
Use: 1 medium-sized bowl, 1 baking tray small enough to fit into your freezer,
and 4 metal cake rings 2$\frac{1}{2}$ inches in diameter.
Serves: 4

SAUCE

1$\frac{1}{2}$ ounces milk chocolate,
preferably 34% cocoa content, broken into pieces

$\frac{1}{4}$ cup heavy cream

1 tablespoon water

1 tablespoon unsalted butter

PIE

melted butter for greasing

4 ounces dark chocolate,
minimum 60% cocoa content, broken into pieces

$\frac{1}{4}$ cup ($\frac{1}{2}$ stick) unsalted butter, unsoftened

$\frac{1}{2}$ cup sugar

2 large eggs, separated, and at room temperature

$\frac{1}{3}$ cup rice flour

$\frac{1}{2}$ cup ground almonds

Melt all the ingredients for the sauce in a saucepan over low heat.

Pour into a freezerproof dish so that the mixture is about an inch deep. Freeze for about six hours or until solid.

Brush a baking tray and the cake rings with the melted butter.

Melt the chocolate in the top of a double boiler over barely simmering water.

Whisk together the butter and sugar until thick and creamy, then add the egg yolks, whisking them into the mixture.

Fold in the rice flour and the ground almonds, then mix in the melted chocolate. In another bowl, whisk the egg whites until stiff peaks form and fold them gently into the mixture.

Place the rings on the baking sheet and use a spoon to fill them a quarter-full with the pie mixture.

Remove the frozen sauce from the freezer. Using a mini metal cutter, cut circles one-inch in diameter from the frozen sauce, and place in the center of each ring. Cover with the pie mixture up to the rim of the ring and then level off with a butter knife. Freeze for at least three hours.

Preheat the oven to 350°F. Remove the baking tray from the freezer and put straight in the oven. Bake for 25 to 30 minutes.

Let the tray cool for five minutes before scraping the excess off the rings. Turn the pies on their sides and gently push the rings off at the bottom.

Serve warm on individual plates.

HINT: Serve with confectioners' sugar, fresh orange segments, or crème fraîche.
Plan in advance and you could serve these with a dusting of pulverised, crystallized orange peel.
You'll find the recipe on page 181.

TIME TO SHINE

Delicious as a filling for crêpes, heated as a sauce with ice cream, or on your toast at breakfast, this sophisticated variation on chocolate spread also makes a lovely gift.

PEAR & CHOCOLATE
SPREAD

Preparation time: 20 minutes
Chilling time: overnight
Cooking time: 40 minutes–1 hour
Use: heavy saucepan, two to three 1½-cup canning jars, wax paper circles
Makes: 1¾ pounds

3 pounds Bartlett pears, ripe but firm

3½ cups granulated sugar

juice of 1 large orange

juice of 1 lemon

9 ounces dark chocolate,
minimum 60% cocoa content, chopped

Peel the pears, cut them into quarters, and remove the cores. In a large heavy saucepan, mix the sugar with the orange and lemon juices, add the pears, and mix together carefully.

Heat gently until the mixture begins to simmer and then remove from the heat and pour into a bowl. Add the chopped chocolate and mix until the chocolate has melted. Cover the bowl, let it cool, and then place in the fridge or leave in a cool place overnight.

Pour the mixture back into a heavy saucepan, bring to a boil and let it bubble for about 40 minutes to an hour, or until the mixture reaches 210°F on a sugar thermometer. (If you do not have one, test by dropping a little onto a cold plate. If it becomes thick and gelatinous, it is ready.)

While the spread is bubbling, wash the canning jars, their lids, and seals in warm soapy water, rinsing thoroughly. Sterilize your jars by immersing them fully in boiling water for 10 minutes. You can also sterilize the jars by washing them in the dishwasher.

Spoon the pear and chocolate spread into the jars to within a half-inch of the rim. Cover with a circle of waxed paper and then immediately put the top on.

HINT: This spread can be stored for up to three months, but once opened, keep in the fridge.

The Lighthouse Bakery in Battersea, southwest London, makes British, European, and American breads and pastries. Elizabeth Weisberg and Rachel Duffield rely on traditional methods of hand-molding, and use long fermentation to develop the full flavor of their dough. They only make Chocolate Bread on Fridays, and on Valentine's Day the bakery makes chocolate heart-shaped rolls.

LIGHTHOUSE
CHOCOLATE BREAD

Preparation: 30 minutes
Proving time: 3 hours
Cooking time: 40 minutes
Use: 1 large baking sheet
Makes: 2 small oval loaves

1 cake fresh yeast or one package active dry yeast

1$^1/_2$ cups minus 2 tablespoons warm water

$^1/_2$ cup sugar

1 large egg yolk

2 tablespoons unsalted butter, softened

4$^1/_2$ cups unbleached white bread flour

1 tablespoon salt

$^1/_3$ cup cocoa powder

9 ounces dark chocolate,
minimum 60% cocoa content, roughly chopped

1 egg yolk for glazing

Combine the yeast, water, and a generous pinch of sugar in a bowl and set aside for 5 to 10 minutes until bubbly. Add the egg yolk and butter to the yeast mixture.

If using a stand mixer, place all the remaining ingredients in the bowl and mix with the paddle for one minute on low speed to combine. Add the yeast mixture and mix with the paddle until well blended. Switch to the dough hook and mix first on low speed and then on medium speed until the dough is smooth and elastic – this takes about four minutes in total. Add a little extra water if it looks too dry.

If working by hand, combine the dry ingredients in a separate bowl and mix briefly with a spoon to blend. Then add the dry ingredients to the yeast mixture in three batches, stirring well with a spoon between additions. Add the chocolate pieces last. Knead the dough on a lightly floured surface for 8 to 10 minutes until the dough is smooth and elastic. Add a little extra water if it looks too dry.

Place the dough in a lightly oiled bowl, cover with plastic wrap and let it prove for about two hours in a warm, draft-free area.

Turn out the dough on to a lightly floured board and punch down. Divide into two equal pieces and shape each into an oval. Place both ovals on a greased or parchment-lined baking sheet, cover with a clean damp dish cloth, and let it prove for about one hour, or until doubled in size.

Preheat the oven to 450°F.

Beat the egg with a fork and brush it over the surface of the loaves. Place them on the baking sheet and bake for 15 minutes. Lower the temperature to 375°F for an additional 25 minutes. Watch the loaves carefully during the last five minutes to avoid scorching the tops. Cool on a wire rack.

HINT: To make the heart shapes, roll the dough into long snakes about one inch in diameter by 15 inches long. Shape into hearts and cut into the top cleavage and inside curves of the heart shape before baking. Make sure you keep an eye on the cooking time as chocolate bread can be ruined easily if baked for too long.

Cocoa is ranked the third most-valued commodity in world food after sugar and coffee. As a result of the pressures of international markets to produce bulk chocolate, there is a wide variety of cocoa beans and, depending on the variety, where they are grown, and how they are processed, they result in many different cocoa flavors.

Cocoa beans are classed as either bulk beans or fine beans. Fine beans are derived from the two best-quality varieties, Criollo and Trinitario. Bulk beans are mainly harvested from the Forastero variety.

The fruit of the cacao tree is an oval-shaped pod about the size of a rugby ball. It can grow as long as 14 inches and weigh up to two and a quarter pounds. When ripe, the pods can be a variety of colors: red, green, orange, or purple.

The word "cacao" (pronounced *kakow*) is derived from the name for the cacao tree, *Theobroma cacao*, and is the word we use before the beans have been fermented and dried. Once dried and ready for shipping, we use the term cocoa.

This wonderful dessert was sent to us by Anne-Marie Graepel. Her mother would rustle this up during the post-war food shortages and it is a delicious chocolate dessert that is simple to make using only ingredients from your pantry. The batter can be refrigerated for up to three days.

CHOCOLATE
LAYERED CRÊPE

Preparation time: 30 minutes
Resting time: 2 hours
Cooking time: 40 minutes
Use: 8-inch heavy crêpe pan, 8- to 9-inch round ovenproof dish,
about 1 to 2 inches deep
Serves: 6–8

CRÊPE BATTER

1$\frac{1}{4}$ cups all-purpose white flour

pinch of salt

$\frac{1}{4}$ cup sugar

3 large eggs

2$\frac{1}{4}$ cups milk

zest of 1 orange

$\frac{1}{3}$ cup plus 1 tablespoon unsalted butter, melted

butter or oil for greasing

FILLING

1$\frac{1}{3}$ cups golden raisins or raisins

1 tablespoon Cointreau

1 tablespoon water

2 heaped tablespoons cocoa powder

5 heaped tablespoons superfine sugar

10$\frac{1}{2}$ ounces apricot jam (about 1 cup)

$\frac{1}{4}$ cup ($\frac{1}{2}$ stick) unsalted butter

1 cup light cream

Soak the raisins in the Cointreau and water. Sift the flour and salt into a bowl, mix in the sugar, and make a well in the center. In a bowl, whisk together the eggs, milk, and orange zest and stir in the melted butter. Pour into the well and, using a whisk, slowly incorporate the flour mixture into the liquid, whisking until smooth and velvety. Pour into a pitcher and let it rest in the fridge for one to two hours.

Before cooking the crêpes, whisk the batter again gently. It should have the consistency of thick cream; if it is too thick, add some milk. Rub a crêpe pan with a little butter or oil and place over medium heat. As soon as the butter begins to bubble, pour in a ladleful of batter. Swirl it evenly around the pan and pour any excess batter back into the pitcher. You will probably need to throw away your first crêpe. Once the crêpe is a nice golden-brown color on the underside, flip it over using a pastry spatula. You will need to keep oiling the pan after two or three crêpes. Pile them, unfolded, on a plate. You should end up with about 20 crêpes.

Preheat the oven to 360°F. Butter the ovenproof dish.

Before layering, first mix the cocoa and sugar in a bowl and have the raisins at hand. Lay a crêpe in the buttered dish, sprinkle with a half-tablespoon of the cocoa mixture and two teasoons of the raisins, lay another crêpe on top, and continue alternating with the cocoa and raisins, and the crêpes, until the fifth crêpe. Spread every fifth crêpe with apricot jam instead of the cocoa and raisins.

When you get to the last crêpe, sprinkle the cocoa and sugar mixture over it and dot with slices of butter. Prick the crêpe pile with a fork and, just before putting it in the oven, pour the cream over the top.

Bake in the oven for 15 minutes until the top layer is nicely crisp. Serve immediately, using a sharp knife to cut into slices.

Nora Carey's passion for preserving was ignited when she worked on the Time Life *Good Cook* series of books while working in London. Nora's food career has ranged from working with Sir Terence Conran at Butler's Wharf, London to Disneyland Resort Paris. Her book, *Perfect Preserves*, is a must for any gardener who loves to cook, and is full of recipes for preserving and using preserves.

CHESTNUT AND CHOCOLATE
SOUFFLÉS

Preparation time: 2 hours including cooling time
Cooking time: 12 minutes
Use: 8 ramekins or custard cups
Serves: 8

1³/₄ cups brown sugar

¹/₂ cup water

14 ounces prepared chestnuts peeled and cooked in water (jars rather than canned)

1 vanilla bean, split lengthwise

¹/₃ cup brandy

¹/₂ cup sugar

14 ounces whole preserved chestnuts in vanilla syrup

8 ounces dark chocolate, minimum 60% cocoa content, broken into pieces

1 cup whole milk

5 tablespoons unsalted butter

3 tablespoons flour

6 large eggs, separated

confectioners' sugar for dusting

Heat the brown sugar with the water over low heat until it begins to boil, add the peeled chestnuts and the vanilla bean. Bring the mixture back to a boil and boil for about three minutes. Let cool for about one hour, then stir in the brandy. Cover with plastic wrap and set aside until needed.

Preheat the oven to 400°F. Brush the ramekins with melted butter and dust with sugar.

Cut the preserved chestnuts in half and divide them between the ramekins.

To make the soufflé, place the chocolate and the milk in a small saucepan over low heat and stir regularly until the chocolate has melted. In a large saucepan, melt the butter, stir in the flour, and cook over low heat, stirring, for about two minutes. When the roux starts to foam, gradually whisk in the chocolate mixture. Cook over medium heat, stirring, for a few minutes until it has thickened. Remove from the heat and let cool. Whisk the egg yolks, one at a time, into the mixture.

In a large bowl, whisk the egg whites until soft peaks form. Gradually whisk in the remaining sugar and continue to whisk until the meringue is firm.

Stir a generous spoonful of the meringue into the chocolate mixture to lighten it, then gently fold the chocolate mixture into the remaining meringue.

Fill the ramekin dishes and bake for 8 to 10 minutes. Do not overfill the soufflés or they will tip over and collapse. Also remember never to open the oven door; if you don't have a light in your oven, peep at them but try not to let too much air into the oven. The soufflés will rise dramatically. Dust with confectioners' sugar and serve immediately before they collapse.

HINT: Horse chestnuts are not edible so, if you are planning to gather your own chestnuts, ensure you have the edible variety (*Castanea sativa*), which have softer spikes than the horse chestnut. If you are roasting your own chestnuts, remember to cut an "X" on the flat side before roasting to prevent explosions.

Lorna Wing is the queen of creative catering and first earned a name for herself doing witty canapés like mini fish and chips in dolly-sized cones made out of the *Financial Times*. This is her twist on Sachertorte that we featured in our very first recipe leaflet in 1993. It has stood the test of time and is the most decadent we have tasted. It also improves over time and is at its best after one week, stored in an airtight container.

LORNA WING'S

SACHERTORTE

Preparation time: 15 minutes
Cooking time: 1 hour
Use: 9-inch springform cake pan
Serves: 10

TORTE

melted butter for greasing

two 3^1/$_2$-oz. bars dark chocolate,
minimum 60% cocoa content, broken into pieces

6 eggs

1^1/$_2$ cups granulated sugar

1^2/$_3$ cups ground almonds

1^1/$_2$ teaspoons freshly ground coffee

6 tablespoons apricot jam

ICING

one 3^1/$_2$-oz. bar dark chocolate,
minimum 60% cocoa content, broken into pieces

3 tablespoons unsalted butter

Preheat the oven to 350°F. Brush the pan with melted butter, then line it with parchment paper. Alternatively, butter the pan and dust with ground almonds to coat.

To make the torte, melt the chocolate in the top of a double boiler over barely simmering water. Separate five of the eggs, then whisk the egg yolks, the whole egg, and the sugar until the mixture is thick and creamy.

In a separate bowl, whisk the egg whites until stiff peaks form.

Add the ground almonds, coffee grounds, and melted chocolate to the egg yolk mixture and stir well. Gently fold in the egg whites and pour into the prepared pan.

Bake for one hour, covering the cake with foil after 40 minutes to prevent the top from burning. Check that a skewer inserted into the center comes out clean and remove the cake from the oven. Release the spring-form ring but leave the cake on the bottom part to cool on a wire rack.

Melt the apricot jam over a low heat, strain, and then brush it over the cooled cake.

To make the icing, melt the chocolate in a heatproof bowl sitting over a saucepan of barely simmering water. Add the butter and stir until it has the consistency of thick pouring cream. Pour the icing evenly over the cake, smoothing it over the top and sides using the back of a teaspoon. Let it set.

HINT: Make a pattern of rings on the top and around the sides of the cake using the back of a teaspoon and then pipe "Sachertorte" in the traditional style.

This recipe comes from Elisabeth Luard, whose mouth-watering article about chocolate made it irresistible and reminds us that wild meat benefits from a sweet-sour marinade and long, gentle cooking. Agrodolce, or sweet & sour sauces, originated in Roman times, when honey, sweet wine, dried fruit, vinegar, and spices were used to mask any unpleasant flavors from the meat, which was not always very fresh, and also to counteract the effects of the preserving salt.

ITALIAN VENISON

AGRODOLCE

Preparation time: 40 minutes
Marinating time: 12 hours minimum
Cooking time: 2 hours
Serves: 6

$3^1/_4$ pound venison (shoulder or haunch), cubed or cut into long strips

MARINADE

$1^3/_4$ cups red wine

3 tablespoons red wine vinegar

3 tablespoons olive oil

1 carrot, chopped

1 large onion, sliced

1 celery stalk including the head, chopped

3 cloves garlic, crushed

sprig rosemary

sprig thyme

4 sage leaves

3 bay leaves

1 teaspoon juniper berries, crushed

$1/_2$ teaspoon black peppercorns, crushed

STEW

3 tablespoons olive oil

$3^1/_2$ ounces pancetta or bacon, diced (about $2/_3$ cup)

1 medium onion, very thinly sliced

1 tablespoon all-purpose flour

1 tablespoon raisins

1 teaspoon ground cinnamon

$1/_2$ teaspoon grated nutmeg

salt and pepper

1-2 tablespoons pine nuts

2-3 squares dark chocolate, minimum 60% cocoa content

Put all the marinade ingredients into a large bowl and stir well. Add the prepared venison and stir, then leave in a cool place overnight, or preferably two nights.

Remove the meat from the marinade and pat dry with paper towels. Strain the marinade and set aside.

Preheat the oven to 300°F.

Heat the oil in a flameproof casserole dish and gently fry the pancetta until the fat runs and it browns a little. Remove and set aside. In the same oil, brown the venison, in batches, to avoid overcrowding the pan. Remove and set aside. Add the onion, season lightly, and cook until soft. Sprinkle in the flour until it absorbs some of the fat, scraping up the caramelized bits. Add the reserved marinade and the raisins, bring to a boil, then reduce the heat and stir until the sauce thickens and no longer smells of alcohol.

Return the pancetta and venison to the casserole dish, let it bubble up, then add the spices, the salt, and the pepper.

Cover and cook in the oven for one and a half hours, until the meat is soft enough to cut with a spoon. Add a little hot water every now and then if it looks as though it is drying out.

Toss the pine nuts in a dry pan over low heat to toast.

When the meat is tender, stir in the dark chocolate and let it bubble up again until the sauce is thick and shiny.

TIME TO SHINE

If you like stollen you will adore this chocolate version created by Liz Usher, who had tried in vain to find a recipe for chocolate bread and decided to create one herself for our National Trust competition. This recipe came a close runner-up to the Chilean chocolate sausages on page 91.

MAYA GOLD

STOLLEN

Soaking time: 12 hours
Preparation time: 30 minutes
Proving time: 30 minutes
Cooking time: 35 minutes
Use: 12 x 8-inch roasting pan
Serves: 10

3 ounces mixed dried fruit, chopped

$^1/_4$ cup candied peel, chopped

$^1/_3$ cup dark rum

zest and juice of 1 orange

one 3$^1/_2$-oz. bar Maya Gold Chocolate, or good-quality dark orange-flavored chocolate

$^1/_3$ cup candied cherries

DOUGH

2$^3/_4$ cups white bread flour

$^1/_4$ cup cocoa powder

$^1/_4$ teaspoon salt

$^1/_2$ teaspoon grated nutmeg

1 teaspoon apple spice

2 teaspoons active dry yeast

$^2/_3$ cup milk

$^1/_2$ cup (1 stick) plus 1 tablespoon unsalted butter

$^1/_4$ cup light brown sugar

2 medium eggs

COCOA MARZIPAN

1 cup ground almonds

$^2/_3$ cup confectioners' sugar

$^1/_4$ cup cocoa powder

DECORATION

$^1/_3$ cup confectioners' sugar

$^1/_4$ cup cocoa powder

Mix the mixed candied fruit and candied peel in half of the rum, and stir in the orange zest and juice. Let soak overnight.

Roughly chop the chocolate into small chunks and quarter the cherries. Mix with the soaked fruits.

To make the dough, combine the flour, cocoa, salt, nutmeg, apple spice, and the yeast.

Gently melt together the milk and a third-cup of the butter, stir in the sugar until dissolved. Let cool. Separate one of the eggs, reserving the white. Beat the yolk with the other egg and whisk into the cooled milk mixture. Make a well in the center of the dry ingredients, add the liquid, and mix well.

Turn out and knead gently on a lightly floured board. Place in the bowl, cover with plastic wrap and leave to rise in a warm place for 30 minutes while you make the marzipan.

Line the roasting pan with parchment paper.

Preheat the oven to 375°F.

HINT: If you like a soft crust on your stollen, place a roasting pan filled with water in the bottom of your oven when you bake it. The steam produced will stop the crust from hardening.

To make the marzipan, mix together the ground almonds, confectioners' sugar, and cocoa with the reserved egg white. Knead lightly together in the bowl until a pliable ball forms. Roll out to an oblong about the length of the pan.

Melt together the remaining butter and rum.

Turn the dough out onto a lightly floured board. Knead a little, then roll it out into an oblong about a quarter-inch thick.

Brush the dough with some melted butter and rum. Place half the fruit mixture on the top two-thirds of the dough, then fold the bottom third, two-thirds of the way up the oblong, then fold down the top third over it. Seal the edges with the rolling pin. Turn the

dough clockwise so that the right-hand edge is now at the bottom, then roll it out into an oblong again. Brush again with the butter and rum and cover the top two-thirds with the remaining fruit mixture, fold, seal, and roll again as before. Do not turn it this time.

Place the marzipan in the center of the dough, fold in the two sides to meet in the center, and place, join-side down, in the lined pan. Brush the top with butter and rum and bake for 35 minutes.

As soon as you remove the stollen from the oven, brush with the remaining butter and rum mixture (which you may need to reheat slightly) and then dredge heavily with confectioners' sugar. Let cool, then sprinkle with cocoa powder for serving.

MELTING

After they have been picked, the pods are carefully cut open with a machete to reveal up to 45 beans surrounded by a gooey, white pulp. The beans and pulp are then removed by hand.

This exquisite tart is from Sue Lawrence's *Book of Baking* which is full of amazingly original recipes including Haggis Bread and an irresistible Rhubarb and White Chocolate Tart.

CHOCOLATE-CRUSTED
LEMON TART

Preparation time: 40 minutes
Chilling time: 3 hours minimum
Cooking time: 35 minutes
Use: 9-inch removable-bottomed fluted tart pan
Serves: 6

PASTRY DOUGH

1 1/4 cups all-purpose flour

1/4 cup cocoa powder

pinch of salt

1/4 cup confectioners' sugar

1/2 cup (1 stick) plus 1 tablespoon unsalted butter, chilled and diced

1 large egg yolk

2 tablespoons cold water

FILLING

3 ounces dark chocolate, minimum 60% cocoa content, grated (about 1 cup)

3 juicy unwaxed lemons

3/4 cup sugar

4 large eggs

2/3 cup heavy cream

confectioners' sugar for sprinkling

To make the pie crust, sift together the flour, cocoa, salt, and confectioners' sugar. Rub in the cold butter using a food processor or your fingertips, until the mixture resembles fine breadcrumbs.

Mix the egg yolk with the water, and add to the mixture to make a dough. You may need a little more water. Gather the dough into a ball, wrap it in waxed paper and chill in the fridge for about one hour.

Roll out the dough from the center and away from you, then back to the center and down towards you, using your weight to push down on it to avoid stretching it. Line the tart pan.

Prick the pie shell with a fork in several places and chill for at least two hours or overnight.

Preheat the oven to 400°F.

Line the pie shell with foil and baking beans and bake blind for 15 minutes, then remove the foil and beans and bake for another five minutes. (Be careful not to overbake as the chocolate crust can quickly develop a bitter taste.) Remove the pan from the oven and reduce the temperature to 350°F.

While the pie crust is still hot, scatter the grated chocolate evenly over the bottom and then let cool.

To make the filling, finely grate the zest from the lemons into a mixing bowl. Squeeze and strain the lemon juice and add it to the zest along with the sugar. Whisk until the sugar has dissolved, then whisk in the eggs and the cream until the mixture is smooth.

Pour the filling into the cooled pie shell and carefully return it to the oven. Bake for 30 to 35 minutes until just set. Remove from the oven and leave on a wire rack to cool completely before removing from the pan.

Dust with confectioners' sugar before serving.

HINT: If you love making pastry dough, try to find yourself a rolling pin with ball bearings in it! You can often pick up large, old ones at flea markets. They are the best because they are heavy, so you don't have to put as much effort into rolling.

MELTING

The pulp that cocoons the deep beet-red, pink, or white beans inside the pod is placed in wooden boxes and lined with banana leaves. They are then covered with more banana leaves and left for about five days to ferment.

The action of fermentation kills the beans and breaks down the sugars whilst other compounds and enzymes react together to produce the precursors of the first chocolate flavors.

Unfermented bulk beans are often used in cheaper chocolate blends where their poor taste can be disguised using additional processing techniques and strong flavors.

Margaret Iveson is a bit of a chocolate addict, along with most of her family and many of her friends. As far as chocolate cakes go, she declares this one is one of the most satisfying and, she also claims, indestructible. Perfect for lazy days like Sundays.

SUNDAY

CHOCOLATE CAKE

Preparation time: 30 minutes
Baking time: 25 minutes
Use: two 8-inch cake pans

1$\frac{1}{2}$ cups all-purpose flour

$\frac{1}{4}$ cup cocoa powder

2 teaspoons baking powder

1 teaspoon baking soda

1 teaspoon lemon juice

scant cup milk

$\frac{1}{3}$ cup plus 1 tablespoon unsalted butter, softened

$\frac{3}{4}$ cup sugar

2 large eggs, beaten

$\frac{1}{2}$ teaspoon vanilla extract

SYRUP

$\frac{1}{4}$ cup apricot jam

2 tablespoons lemon juice

1 tablespoon kirsch

BUTTER CREAM FILLING

one 3$\frac{1}{2}$-oz. bar dark chocolate, minimum 60% cocoa content

$\frac{1}{4}$ cup ($\frac{1}{2}$ stick) unsalted butter

1 cup confectioners' sugar

1 large egg yolk

ICING

2 ounces dark chocolate, minimum 60% cocoa content

2 tablespoons unsalted butter

1 tablespoon rum

Preheat the oven to 375°F. Butter and flour the cake pans.

Sift together the flour, cocoa, baking powder, and baking soda three times.

Stir the lemon juice into the milk to curdle it.

In a large bowl, cream together the softened butter and sugar until fluffy. Beat in some of the egg, then some of the flour mixture, then some of the milk and lemon juice. Continue in this way, beating vigorously between each addition, until the batter is fairly stiff (don't add all the milk if it seems to be getting too liquid). Finally add the vanilla extract.

Divide the batter between the pans and bake for 20 to 25 minutes, until springy to the touch. Leave the cakes in their pans for a few minutes and then turn them out to cool on to a wire rack, so that the top crust is on the bottom. Prick the bottoms gently all over.

To make the syrup, simmer the jam, lemon juice, and kirsch and pour it evenly over the cooled cakes.

For the Butter Cream Filling, melt the chocolate in the top of a double boiler over barely simmering water and let cool until warm to the touch while you cream together the butter and confectioners' sugar. Beat in the egg yolk, then the chocolate, spread it onto the cake surfaces and sandwich the cakes together.

To make the icing, melt the chocolate as above, beat in the butter, then the rum, and continue to beat until glossy. Let cool slightly before pouring over the top of the cake. Let it set.

MELTING

The only drink for a very hot summer's day or on a balmy night – sip and feel yourself cool down. Iced Mocha Coffee is also perfect as a dessert after a barbecue or *al fresco* lunch.

ICED

MOCHA

Preparation time: 15–20 minutes
Marinating time: 8 hours minimum, or up to 1 week
Chilling time: 2 hours
Makes: 6 tall glasses

7 ounces (about 1 cup) fresh cherries

1¼ cups brandy or port

4 cups strong, freshly ground, brewed coffee

½ cup good-quality hot chocolate powder

6 tablespoons demerara (raw) sugar

2¼ cups dark chocolate ice cream

2¼ cups vanilla ice cream

1 cup heavy cream

cocoa powder or dark chocolate for sprinkling

Marinate the cherries in the brandy or port overnight, or preferably for up to one week, in the fridge.

Make the coffee and while it is still hot stir in the hot chocolate and the sugar to taste. Remember not to make the mocha too sweet as the ice cream will be an additional sweetener.

Chill the mocha in the fridge until very cold. Remove the ice cream from the freezer and let soften for 10 minutes. Pour the mocha into six glasses, only three-quarters full, to allow enough room for two balls of ice cream.

Drop three or four marinated cherries into each glass and then, using an ice cream scoop, carefully drop one ball of vanilla ice cream into the mocha, then one ball of chocolate ice cream on top. Try not to disturb the ice cream too much as it will cloud the lovely dark mocha coffee. Pour one to two tablespoons of cream over the top of the ice cream and then sprinkle some cocoa or dark chocolate flakes over it. Serve immediately.

HINT: You can use leftover brewed coffee, but if it has cooled, don't reheat it. Just pour a little hot water over the hot chocolate powder before you add it to the coffee. If it is an unbearably hot day, put some ice cubes into the mocha before you add the ice cream.

Sylvia Sacco made this tiramisu for the end-of-filming party for Gilly Booth's film *One Dau Trois 123*, in which Sylvia played the leading lady. The recipe belongs to her mother, Sonia Nicastro, and lives up to its name, which means "pick-me-up." The exhausted film crew couldn't get enough of it and the recipe was immediately nabbed for this book.

SYLVIA'S

TIRAMISU

Preparation time: 25 minutes
Chilling time: minimum 2 hours or overnight
Use: 9-inch serving dish, about 3 inches deep
Serves: 6

7 ounces Savoiardi cookies or ladyfingers

1$^1/_2$ cups espresso or strong brewed coffee

$^1/_4$ cup Grand Marnier or Marsala

4 eggs, separated

$^1/_2$ cup granulated sugar

14 ounces mascarpone cheese

pinch of salt

2 tablespoons cocoa powder

Break the cookies into two or three pieces and line the bottom of the serving dish with half of them. Spoon half the coffee over the cookies and then drizzle them with half of the liqueur.

Whisk together the egg yolks and sugar until thick and creamy, add the mascarpone cheese, and stir well until smooth and thick. Whisk the egg whites until stiff peaks form and add a pinch of salt. Gently fold the egg whites into the mascarpone cheese and egg mixture.

Spoon half the mixture over the cookies in the bottom of the dish. Place the remaining cookies on top of the mixture, spoon the reserved coffee over them, and then drizzle with the rest of the liqueur. Cover with the remaining mascarpone cheese and egg mixture. Sift the cocoa powder evenly over the top.

Cover with plastic wrap and chill for at least two hours, or preferably overnight.

HINT: Tiramisu is traditionally served in a glass bowl, but why not be adventurous and use a terracotta dish? It also looks beautiful in an old china vegetable serving dish.

Deryl Rennie made this loaf cake so that she could enjoy her two favourite flavors at once. The pieces of chocolate sink into the batter so that they embed themselves at the bottom of the loaf while the lemon gives the cake a refreshing edge.

LEMON DRIZZLE

WITH SUNKEN DARK CHOCOLATE CHUNKS

Preparation time: 15 minutes
Cooking time: 40 minutes
Use: 5 x 7-inch loaf pan
Serves: 10

BATTER

$^1/_2$ cup (1 stick) plus 1 tablespoon unsalted butter

$^1/_2$ cup sugar

2 large eggs

1 cup self-rising flour

1 teaspoon baking powder

grated rind of 1 large lemon

1 tablespoon milk

3 ounces dark chocolate, minimum 60% cocoa content, chopped

LEMON DRIZZLE

$^1/_4$ cup light brown sugar

juice of 1 lemon

Preheat the oven to 350°F. Line the loaf pan with parchment paper. Alternatively, butter the pan and dust with flour to coat. Shake out the excess flour.

Whisk the butter, sugar, eggs, flour, baking powder, and lemon rind together for about two minutes. Whisk in the milk to make a soft dropping consistency. Stir in the chocolate.

Spoon the mixture into the prepared pan, smooth the surface, and bake for 40 minutes or until the center of the cake springs back when gently pressed. Remove from the oven.

Stir the light brown sugar into the lemon juice and pour it over the hot cake in its pan. Make a few holes with a fine skewer if the lemon icing remains on the surface.

Remove the cake from its pan and place on a wire rack, leaving it in its paper (if using) to cool completely.

HINT: If you use grated chocolate, it will give the cake a speckly appearance.

A fun way to serve this sorbet is with a glass of coffee liqueur which can then be poured over the sorbet or drunk separately. It is equally delicious served with a delicate *crème anglaise* and perfectly ripe peaches, raspberries, oranges, nectarines, or apricots, and simple butter cookies or tuiles.

CHOCOLATE

SORBET

Preparation time: 15 minutes
Freezing time: 3–4 hours
Use: ice cream machine
Serves: 4

one 3$\frac{1}{2}$-oz. bar dark chocolate,
minimum 60% cocoa content, broken into pieces

$\frac{1}{2}$ cup water

$\frac{2}{3}$ cup cocoa powder

SUGAR SYRUP

1 cup water

$\frac{2}{3}$ cup sugar

To prepare the sugar syrup, put the sugar and the water into a saucepan and bring to a boil without stirring, let it bubble for about five minutes or until the sugar has dissolved, then remove from the heat.

While the sugar syrup is bubbling, melt the chocolate in the top of a double boiler over barely simmering water. Once it has melted, add the half-cup of water to the sugar syrup and reheat until warm, whisk in the cocoa, then add the melted chocolate, whisking together until smooth.

Churn in an ice cream maker, following the manufacturer's instructions, until smooth.

HINT: It is a good idea to cool the sorbet down before churning it, since it will set more quickly if cool.
To do this, place it over a bowl of water filled with ice cubes and stir occasionally,
but be careful not to let any of the water into the sorbet at this stage.

MELTING

There are few commercially made ice creams that are a patch on the homemade version and the key to this is in the stirring and cooling, as well as the ingredients. It is vital to have an ice cream machine to achieve a thick, creamy texture, and to use the best-quality eggs and dairy products.

ICE CREAM

Preparation time: 15 minutes
Chilling time: 10-20 minutes
Use: ice cream maker
Serves: 6

1 cup whole milk

1¼ cups heavy cream

1 vanilla bean

3 large egg yolks

½ cup sugar

Pour the milk and cream into a heavy saucepan. Split the vanilla bean lengthwise, scrape out the seeds, and add both the bean and seeds to the milk and cream mixture. Bring to a boil, then remove from the heat, cover, and let infuse for about 15 minutes. Strain the liquid.

Beat the egg yolks and sugar until thick and creamy. Continue to beat as you pour in a little of the strained milk and cream, then add the rest of the milk and cream and beat until well blended. Place the saucepan over medium heat and, stirring frequently with a wooden spoon, cook until the custard has thickened and coats the back of the spoon. Then follow your chosen recipe below.

CHOCOLATE, HAZELNUT, & CURRANT

one 3½-oz. bar dark chocolate,
minimum 60% cocoa content, broken into pieces

one 3½-oz. bar Hazelnut and Currant Chocolate,
or other good-quality fruit and nut chocolate,
finely chopped

Melt the dark chocolate in the top of a double boiler over barely simmering water and carefully stir it into the already-prepared custard.

Transfer the chocolate custard to a metal bowl and place the bowl on a bed of ice in a little water to chill. Stir occasionally to prevent a skin from forming.

Once the custard has cooled, transfer to an ice cream machine and churn according to the manufacturer's instructions. Add the chunks of Hazelnut and Currant Chocolate just before the ice cream sets.

CARAMEL BAR

one 3½-oz. bar Caramel Chocolate, or any other
flavored bar, chopped into medium-sized chunks

Remove from the heat, transfer to a metal bowl, and place it on a bed of ice and a little water to chill. Stir occasionally to prevent a skin from forming. Once the custard has cooled add the chunks of caramel chocolate, transfer to the ice cream machine, and churn according to the manufacturer's instructions.

SAUCES

CARAMEL BAR

one 3¹/₂-oz. bar Caramel Chocolate, broken into pieces

1 tablespoon cream or milk

Melt the chocolate in the top of a double boiler over barely simmering water. Remove from the heat and stir in the cream or milk. Let it cool for a few minutes and then pour it over cake or use as a sauce for ice cream.

SIMPLE CHOCOLATE

one 3¹/₂-oz. bar dark chocolate, minimum 60% cocoa content, chopped

¹/₂ cup heavy or whipping cream

1 tablespoon unsalted butter

Melt the chocolate along with the cream in the top of a double boiler over barely simmering water, stirring frequently. Once the chocolate has melted, add the butter and stir until it has melted. Serve warm.

ALISTAIR LITTLE'S CHOCOLATE FUDGE

¹/₂ cup heavy cream

²/₃ cup sugar

2 tablespoons unsalted butter

¹/₃ cup golden syrup or corn syrup

¹/₃ cup milk

¹/₂ teaspoon vanilla extract

one 3¹/₂-oz. bar dark chocolate, minimum 60% cocoa content, broken into pieces

Put all the ingredients, except the chocolate, in a heavy saucepan over medium heat, stirring constantly until the mixture is a pale caramel color. This will take about 10 to 15 minutes after coming to a slow boil. Remove from the heat and beat in the chocolate pieces. Stir in three tablepoons of cold water. If the mixture is still too thick, continue adding water, a spoonful at a time, until you achieve a good pouring consistency. Serve immediately or keep warm in a water bath until needed.

CUSTARD

1 vanilla bean

1¹/₄ cups whole milk

2 large egg yolks (3 if you want a very thick sauce)

1 heaped tablespoon sugar

Split the vanilla bean lengthwise, scrape out the seeds, and put both bean and seeds in a saucepan along with the milk. Bring to a boil and then remove from the heat and let infuse for 15 minutes. Beat the egg yolks and sugar until thick and creamy. Remove the vanilla bean and reheat the milk until it begins to boil, then whisk the boiling milk into the egg mixture. Pour it back into the saucepan and heat gently, stirring all the time with a wooden spoon, until the sauce begins to thicken, and dragging your finger or a knife across the back of the spoon leaves a clear trail. Remove the custard from the heat and pour into a bowl. Serve hot or chilled.

CUSTARD WITH MINT

Make the recipe as above but substitute the vanilla bean with a handful of chopped mint. Add Crème de menthe to taste once the custard has cooled a little.

LICKING THE BOWL

With the only high school far away in Punta Gorda, many cacao farmers' children have to board with families near the school. Without the extra income generated from Fairtrade organically grown cacao, their parents would not be able to afford the cost of their accommodation and the weekly bus fare.

LICKING THE BOWL

Here is a good way to feed hordes of children a dessert that they all love without having piles of bowls to wash up. Make it extra naughty by filling the bottom with a surprise: jelly beans, malted milk balls, M&Ms, Rolos, silver balls, or any other chocolate candy. Don't tempt them by telling them the surprise is there, otherwise they'll bite the bottom and you will wonder why you didn't give them the bowls!

FRUIT SPLIT

SURPRISE

Preparation time: 15 minutes
Use: a block of styrofoam to hold the dipped cones

milk chocolate bars, for dipping the cones

chopped nuts or silver balls or candy shots for coating the chocolate-dipped cones

quality wafer ice cream cones

chocolate and vanilla ice cream

YOUR CHOICE OF:

melon, cut into tall slices

bananas, cut in half

pineapple, cut into long tall chunks

dragon fruit, sliced into quarters, skin on

kiwi fruit, sliced lengthwise

your choice of candies that will fit into the bottom of the cone

drinking chocolate powder, for decorating

Remove the ice cream from the freezer and let it soften for 10 minutes. Melt the chocolate in the top of a double boiler over barely simmering water.

Dip the tops of the cones in the melted chocolate and then into the chopped nuts, silver balls, or candy shots. Wedge the point of the cone into a large piece of styrofoam to set.

Fill the bottoms of the cones with a few candies. Then place softened ice cream down one side of the cone and your slices of fruit down the other side of the cone so that they stick out at the top. Wedge more ice cream into the cone to help hold the fruit up, then sprinkle with the chocolate powder.

HINT: You can make this treat even naughtier by wedging a half of a chocolate finger in the cone as well.

Bea Hovell is seven years old and she loves baking. She usually makes her Thumbprint Cookies with jam as a filling, but has found that our chocolate spread seems to be another perfect partner for them. Remember chocolate spread has hazelnuts in it so do be careful who you give them to!

BEA'S

THUMBPRINT COOKIES

Preparation time: 20 minutes
Resting time: 1 hour
Cooking time: 10–12 minutes
Makes: 18–24

$^3/_4$ cup (1$^1/_2$ sticks) unsalted butter, softened

$^3/_4$ cup sugar

1 large egg

1 cup self-rising flour

1$^1/_3$ cups all-purpose flour

7 ounces chocolate hazelnut spread (about 1 cup)

Line a baking sheet with parchment paper or else grease it well with butter.

Cream the butter and sugar until light and fluffy using an electric beater. Add the egg and beat well. Stir in the two flours and mix to a dough. Let it rest for one hour.

Preheat the oven to 350°F.

Use the palms of your hands to roll about one heaped tablespoon of the dough into a ball about an inch in diameter, then use the palm of your hand to flatten it onto the baking sheet. Press your thumb into the middle of the dough to make a hole. Continue with the rest of the dough, ensuring the cookies are spaced far enough apart to let them expand as they cook. Using a teaspoon, fill each hole with the chocolate spread.

Bake for 10 to 12 minutes or until the cookies are golden. Cool on a wire rack.

HINT: Place a dishtowel under the bowl to prevent it from slipping while you are beating, and, if using parchment paper, put four little dots of butter on the baking tray before you line it with the paper to stop the paper from shifting.

After fermentation, the beans are spread out on mats to dry in the sun and raked over intermittently. In sunny weather, drying the beans usually takes about a week.

LICKING THE BOWL

One of the toughest challenges of chocolate baking is to make a healthy birthday cake for children that they will enjoy, but won't send them into a sugar-induced spin. Here, instead of sweet frosting and decorations, an imaginative use of fruit provides all the color and shape you will need. Of course you can also add candies and chocolate decorations once they are older – after all, what are birthdays for? Kids will also love creating a design – encourage them to come up with ideas for shapes and decoration.

FRUITY FISH
BIRTHDAY CAKE

Preparation time: 20 minutes
Baking time: 35 minutes, depending on the pan you use
Use: 12 x 11-inch roasting pan or round cake pans
depending on the shape you need for your cake, and a large tray for serving
Serves: 15 (double the recipe and use two roasting pans if you want to make a cake
as large as the one in the photograph, which serves 30)

CAKE

12 eggs, separated

1³/₄ cups sugar

1¹/₂ cups all-purpose flour, sifted

1 cup good-quality cocoa powder

³/₄ cup (1¹/₂ sticks) unsalted butter, melted and cooled

TOPPING SUGGESTIONS

Thick whole-milk yogurt mixed with a little honey or a smooth fruit compote are healthier alternatives to sugary frostings.

Chocolate spread is another good quick, sticky topping for older children, but don't forget that it includes hazelnuts!

Chocolate bars melted with one tablespoon heavy cream per bar – try caramel chocolate for extra indulgence.

DECORATION

Quantities of different fruits of all colors and shapes. (Try slices of kiwi fruit for a cat's eyes, segments of orange or clementines for fish scales.)

Candies, wafer fans, licorice shoe strings or ropes, ice cream cones, Life savers.

Toys and miniature figures.

Toothpicks and skewers are great for holding things together.

HINT: Since you are making this cake at home and don't have to worry about transporting it, you can be as ambitious and extravagant as you please. Why not try three-dimensional designs?

To make the cake, preheat the oven to 350°F. Line the baking pans with parchment paper. Alternatively, butter the pans and dust with flour to coat.

Beat the egg yolks with the sugar until thick and creamy. The mixture should be pale, and when you lift the beater above the bowl, it should fall from the beater in a thick ribbon. Beat the egg whites until light and fluffy. Sift the flour and the cocoa together and then fold in, in three or four stages, alternating with the beaten whites and the melted, cooled butter.

Pour the batter into the prepared pans and bake in the oven for about 35 minutes for a deep cake, about 20 minutes for a shallow one, and 5 to 10 minutes if you are using a roasting pan. Once you begin to smell it cooking, take a look. To test whether the cake is done, insert a skewer into the center and press the top of the cake. If the skewer comes out clean, and if the cake is springy and the edges have come away from the sides of the pan, it is done.

Leave the cake in the pan for a few minutes and then turn it out onto a wire rack to cool before removing the parchment paper, if using.

To decorate, find a picture or figure of a character or scene to use as a guide. By studying it, you will find little details that will be easy to replicate using pieces of cake or fruit.

Prepare a large serving tray by covering it with foil.

Place the cake on a wooden board and, with a bread knife, cut it to your desired shape. You don't have to make the shape from one piece of cake, and you can easily stick bits of cake together using chocolate spread or some other "mortar". Assemble your shape on the tray.

Frost the cake with your chosen topping, then let your imagination run wild. Try to group the same fruits together in blocks of color to create a cake that children will adore.

Penny Parker gives heavenly teas and has many recipes that people are always asking for, which she is very happy to pass along. We are always surprised by the number of people who have sent us improvized recipes because their friend would not give them the original. These Chocolate Oat Bars are the original recipe and contain muscovado sugar, which gives them a rich flavor and takes the edge off the usual sweetness inherent in oat bars.

CHOCOLATE
OAT BARS

Preparation time: 10 minutes
Baking time: 20 minutes
Use: 7 x 11-inch baking tray or roasting pan
Makes: 20

1¹/₂ cups (3 sticks) unsalted butter

3 tablespoons golden syrup or corn syrup

³/₄ cup soft brown sugar

³/₄ cup muscovado sugar (if available, use soft brown sugar)

1¹/₂ cups good-quality oats (oat flakes)

3 cups processed oats (rolled or porridge oats)

6 tablespoons good-quality cocoa powder

Preheat the oven to 275°F. Butter the baking tray.

Melt the butter, syrup, and both sugars in a large saucepan. Do not let them bubble. Mix in the oats and the cocoa until thoroughly combined.

Tip the contents of the saucepan into the buttered baking tray and, using a fork, press the mixture into the baking tray until it's evenly flat. Bake for 18 to 20 minutes. The oat bars need to cook to the center but you don't want them to bubble, otherwise they will be too toffee-like. They should stay moist.

Remove from the oven and let cool for about 20 minutes before slicing up. Let cool completely before removing from the tray.

HINT: These oat bars are delicious with two tablespoons of dried shredded coconut, or a handful of golden raisins added with the oats. Equally tasty is one tablespoon of sesame seeds, but you will also need a handful of extra oats because the seeds will make the oat bars oily.

Fun to make and adored by children, you only have to look at the ingredients to see why. These balls of chocolate caramel are a recipe from jewelry designer, Valerie Black, and one which reminds her of her childhood in Argentina. Adjust the cocoa to taste and cover the Brigadeiros in anything from confectioners' sugar to chocolate sprinkles. Adults with a sweet tooth love them with a dusting of cocoa.

BRIGADEIROS

Preparation time: 15 minutes
Cooking time: 30 minutes
Cooling time: 2 hours

one 14-oz. can of condensed milk

2–3 tablespoons cocoa powder

unsalted butter for greasing

confectioners' sugar, chocolate sprinkles, silver balls, or other covering

To make the caramel, pour the condensed milk into a saucepan, add cocoa to taste, and place over medium heat. Stir the caramel regularly and with care because it will be very hot. Once it begins to thicken, stir continuously until the caramel separates as you drag the spoon through it.

This will take about 30 minutes. Remove from the heat and set aside to cool for about two hours.

Sift the confectioners' sugar into a bowl. Once the mixture has cooled, rub some butter on your hands and, taking a spoonful of mixture at a time, roll it into balls in your palms, then drop each one into the powdered sugar, chocolate sprinkles, or silver balls, moving it from hand to hand to dust off any excess.

Arrange on a decorative platter and serve.

HINT: Keep children away from the hot caramel as it can cause serious burns.

This recipe has sweet memories for Sandra Halliwell as it reminds her of "Poor Night's Supper" or the bread, butter, and jam her father used to make. During these meals, her sister used to tell tales of knights in shining armor, sitting down to their own "Poor Knight's Supper."

SWEET
MEMORIES

Preparation time: 20 minutes
Deep-frying time: 1–2 minutes each
Use: deep-fat fryer or saucepan for deep frying
Makes: 12 triangles

BATTER

1 cup flour

pinch of salt

1 teaspoon ground cinnamon

1 egg

$^2/_3$ cup milk

SWEET MEMORIES

6 slices white bread

6 teaspoons raspberry conserve

$^1/_2$ cup shredded cheddar cheese

$2^1/_2$ ounces milk chocolate,
preferably 34% cocoa content, chopped

2 cups vegetable oil

2 tablespoons confectioners' sugar

To make the batter, sift the flour, salt, and cinnamon into a bowl. Make a well in the center, drop in the egg, gradually add half the milk and mix to a smooth batter, using a wooden spoon to draw in the flour from the sides. Add the rest of the milk and beat the batter for 5 to 10 minutes until it is thoroughly aerated. Leave it in a cool place until needed.

Take three slices of the bread and cover each one with the raspberry conserve, the cheese, and the chocolate. Place the remaining three slices on top to make three sandwiches. Press down well to seal in the filling and cut each sandwich into four triangles. Dip into the batter.

Heat the vegetable oil in a deep-fat fryer or in a saucepan until it is smoking hot. Carefully place a few sandwich triangles into the fat, remembering it might spit.

Once they have browned, turn them over until they are a golden-brown color on both sides. The triangles will expand in the fat so cook them in batches.

Remove and drain the triangles on crumpled paper towels. Sift the confectioners' sugar and cinnamon over the Sweet Memories before serving.

HINT: Be careful not to leave the hot fat in the saucepan within easy reach of children.

LICKING THE BOWL

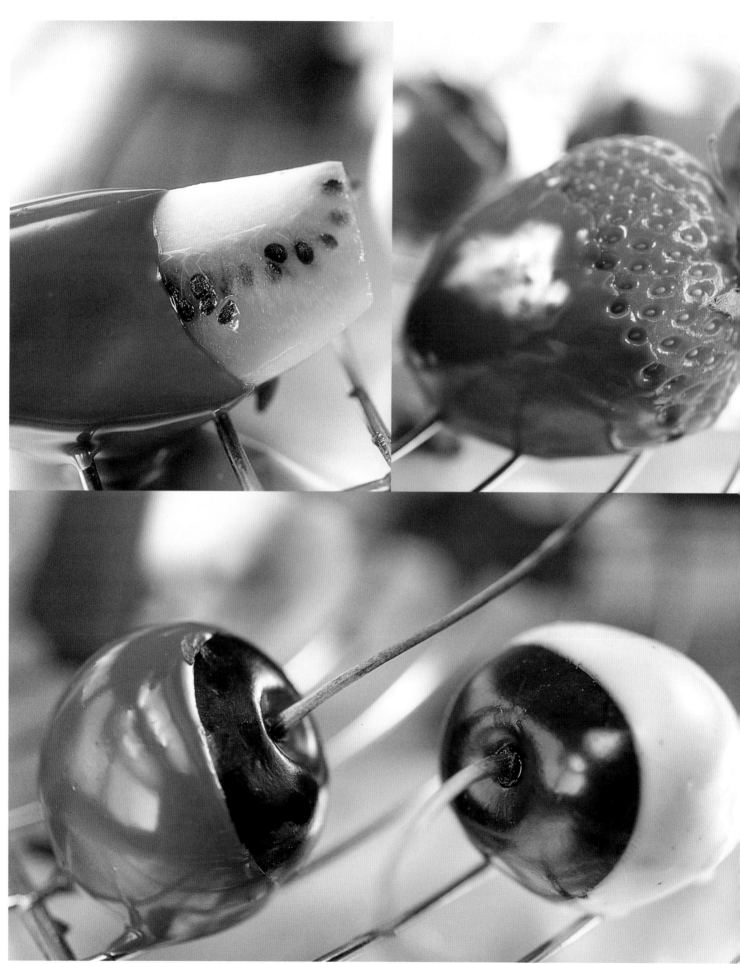

Haley Foxen is the goddaughter of our founder, Josephine Fairley. Haley's mother was the chairman of the Soil Association and, along with Jo and Craig Sams, was a driving force in the campaign for the return to farming methods that work in harmony with nature and that produce food with real taste. Haley gave us this recipe when Green & Black's was first launched.

CHOCOLATE
DIPPED FRUIT

Preparation time: 30 minutes
Use: wire rack, or toothpicks and a block of styrofoam, or two halves of a watermelon to support the dipped fruit
Makes: about 100 pieces

one 3$\frac{1}{2}$-oz. bar milk chocolate, preferably 34% cocoa content, broken into pieces

one 3$\frac{1}{2}$-oz. bar good-quality white chocolate, broken into pieces

one 3$\frac{1}{2}$-oz. bar Maya Gold, or a good-quality, dark, orange-flavored chocolate, broken into pieces

12 strawberries, stems in place

2 ripe kiwi fruit, sliced

12 cherries, stalks in place

1 pineapple, cut into triangular pieces

2 bananas, sliced at an angle

2 mangoes, sliced

1 carton Cape gooseberries (also known as physallis)

2 dragon fruit (a Vietnamese red-skinned cactus fruit), sliced into quarters, skin on

Melt the three chocolates separately in heatproof bowls each sitting over its own saucepan of barely simmering water. Take extra care with the white chocolate: you may want to melt it over a saucepan of boiled water off the heat. Let cool for about five minutes before dipping the fruit.

You can use toothpicks to skewer the prepared fruit, dipping the pieces so that each one is half-covered with chocolate, then stick them in the styrofoam or watermelon to set. Alternatively, hold the fruit with your fingers, dip them into the chocolate and let them set on a wire rack. Continue until all the chocolate is used up.

Once dipped, do not put the fruit in the fridge otherwise the chocolate will lose its shine.

HINT: You can also freeze the prepared fruit before dunking it in the chocolate and then return it to the freezer on a tray lined with waxed paper for a sweltering, summer's day treat.

Why buy a muffin made with heavily-processed ingredients and artificial flavors when the real thing can be made so easily at home? These muffins are ideal for older children to make by themselves and can be eaten soon after they are removed from the oven.

BANANA, CHERRY, AND WHITE CHOCOLATE

MUFFINS

Preparation time: 10 minutes
Cooking time: 20 minutes
Use: paper muffin cups or a 10-cup muffin tray
Makes: 10 large muffins

1 cup all-purpose flour

$\frac{1}{2}$ tablespoon baking powder

$\frac{1}{4}$ teaspoon salt

1 medium egg

3 tablespoons caster sugar

$\frac{1}{2}$ cup milk

$\frac{1}{4}$ cup ($\frac{1}{2}$ stick) unsalted butter, melted

2 ounces dried cherries, chopped (about $\frac{1}{4}$ cup)

2 ounces white chocolate, chopped (about $\frac{1}{3}$ cup)

1 small banana, mashed

Preheat the oven to 400°F.

Sift together the flour, baking powder, and salt. In a separate bowl whisk together the egg, sugar, milk, and melted butter. Mix the dry ingredients into the wet ingredients. Don't try to blend them too evenly — they should remain a little lumpy. Add the cherries, white chocolate, and mashed banana and stir, but again, do not overmix.

Spoon into the paper muffin cups or muffin tray, filling each approximately two-thirds full.

Bake for 20 minutes.

HINT: The muffin batter should not be evenly blended otherwise the muffins will have too smooth a texture and will be more like cupcakes.

The perfect after-supper dessert served with fruit salad. Children love to do the flipping and watch the drop scones magically change their form. Ensure that they use giant oven mitts so that they don't get hit by any stray spits of fat, and make sure someone is there to hold the pan.

CHOCOLATE
DROP SCONES

Preparation time: 15 minutes
Cooking time: 20 minutes
Use: heavy frying pan and spatula
Makes: 18–20

³/₄ cup self-rising flour

1 teaspoon baking powder

3 tablespoons sugar

¹/₄ cup cocoa powder

1 large egg

²/₃ cup milk

¹/₃ cup (³/₄ stick) unsalted butter

Grated zest of 1 orange or
teaspoon grated fresh ginger (optional)

Sift the flour, baking powder, sugar, and cocoa into a large bowl. Make a well in the center and drop in the egg. Beat the egg, gradually drawing in the flour. Slowly add the milk a little at a time, mixing the ingredients to form a smooth batter the consistency of thick pouring cream. Keep your actions gentle otherwise the drop scones will be tough.

Stir in one of the optional flavorings if you like.

Melt the butter in the frying pan over low heat and then pour it into a heat-resistant measuring cup and keep it by the stove.

Test the frying pan's temperature by cooking one drop scone first. Pour a tablespoon or so of the batter onto the hot, greased pan. Let it cook until a few bubbles appear on the surface and burst, then flip it, and let it cook on the other side for one minute.

If the pan seems hot enough, then continue to cook the remaining drop scones in the same way, cooking three at a time and leaving lots of space between them so they don't run together. Add more melted butter to the pan between batches and make sure the entire surface of the pan is greased before pouring in the next batch.

Add more melted butter to the pan between batches and ensure it covers the surface fully before cooking the next batch.

Serve immediately with butter, chocolate spread, sprinkled with sugar and a squeeze of lemon juice, or with jam and a dollop of cream.

HINT: To reheat, wrap in layers of aluminum foil and place in a warm oven for a few minutes.

CREATE A STIR

The dried beans must contain less than seven to eight percent moisture,
to prevent mold growth during storage.

These will surprise you and only get better as you devour them and the heat of the chiles takes hold. Chile is one of the oldest partners for chocolate and this is a great way to eat them, and a wonderfully unusual treat. Helen Garmston, one of the runners-up in our *Country Living* magazine recipe competition, first made these muffins as a dessert for a Mexican buffet supper. They are equally good for breakfast or brunch.

MEXICAN MOLE
MUFFINS

Preparation time: 15 minutes
Baking time: 20 minutes
Use: 12-cup muffin pan, 24 paper muffin cups
Makes: 12 muffins

one 3$\frac{1}{2}$-oz. bar milk chocolate, preferably 34% cocoa content

$\frac{1}{2}$ ounce or more fresh red chiles (thumb- or finger-length chiles are likely to be medium hot), finely diced (about 2 tablepoons)

1$\frac{1}{2}$ cups all-purpose flour

$\frac{1}{4}$ cup good-quality cocoa powder

1 teaspoon baking powder

$\frac{1}{2}$ teaspoon salt

$\frac{1}{2}$ cup sugar

2 medium eggs

$\frac{1}{2}$ cup sunflower oil

1 cup milk

1 teaspoon vanilla extract

Preheat the oven to 400°F. Line a 12-cup muffin pan with double paper muffin cups.

Coarsely grate the milk chocolate. Finely dice the red chiles, discarding the seeds and membrane, being careful not to touch the flesh of the chiles. It is best to use rubber gloves.

Sift the flour, cocoa, baking powder, and salt into a bowl, and stir in the sugar, grated chocolate, and diced chile. Make a well in the center.

In another bowl, beat the eggs and sunflower oil until foamy, then gradually beat in the milk and vanilla extract. Pour the dry ingredients into the well and stir until just combined. Don't be tempted to overmix, otherwise they will not have the rough texture of a traditional muffin.

Spoon the mixture into the paper cups, filling each three-quarters full. Bake for approximately 20 minutes, until the muffins are well-risen and springy.

Let the muffins cool in the pan for a few minutes and serve them warm, or turn them onto a wire rack to cool completely.

HINT: If you do touch the flesh of the chiles with your bare hands, be extra careful not to touch your eyes.

The beets in this cake give it a moist, velvety texture and just a hint of a purple color. It is very beety when you first eat it and then the flavor becomes less shocking as time goes by! Most cakes with vegetables in them were first made because of a surplus of home-grown vegetables. Vicki van Esch sent us this version, adapted from an Australian recipe.

CHOCOLATE
BEET CAKE

Preparation time: 30 minutes
Cooking time: 50 minutes
Use: 7-inch round cake pan
Makes: 8 slices

1 cup presweetened cocoa powder

1³/₄ cups self-rising flour

1 cup light brown sugar

one 3¹/₂-oz. bar dark chocolate, minimum 60% cocoa content, broken into pieces

¹/₂ cup (1 stick) unsalted butter

9 ounces cooked beets (about 1¹/₂ cups)

3 large eggs

FOR SERVING

confectioners' sugar for dusting

crème fraîche

Preheat the oven to 350°F.

Butter and flour the cake pan, and shake out any excess flour.

Sift together the presweetened cocoa and the self-rising flour, then mix in the sugar. Melt the chocolate and butter together in the top of a double boiler over barely simmering water. Purée the beets in a food processor, whisk the eggs, then stir them into the puréed beets. Add the beet and the chocolate mixtures to the dry ingredients and mix together thoroughly.

Pour the mixture into the cake pan. Bake for 50 minutes or until a skewer inserted into the center comes out clean. Remove from the oven and let the cake remain in its pan for 10 minutes before turning it out onto a wire rack to cool. Serve dusted with confectioners' sugar and some crème fraîche.

HINT: To give the cake a dramatic topping, you could grate some cooked beets and add them to a standard white frosting. Remember to use rubber gloves when handling the beets – they stain the skin!

Delicate hands are needed for this hedonistic dessert sent to us by Phillip Harris-Jones, who grows his own chiles. Late one night towards the end of a dinner party, he served thinly sliced chiles that had been marinating in vodka with a bar of Green & Black's Dark Chocolate; one thing led to another and his next dinner-party guests enjoyed these unforgettable chocolates.

VODKA CHILE

CHOCOLATES

Marinating time: 12 hours
Preparation time: 30 minutes
Use: pastry bag and small nozzle
Makes: 12 chile chocolates

6 green chile peppers, stalks on

6 red chile peppers, stalks on

1$\frac{1}{2}$ cups vodka

one 3$\frac{1}{2}$-oz. bar good-quality white chocolate or dark chocolate, minimum 60% cocoa content, to fill the chiles

black pepper, freshly ground

confectioners' sugar and black pepper, for serving

FOR DIPPING

one 3$\frac{1}{2}$-oz. bar dark chocolate, minimum 60% cocoa content

Wash the chiles, then cut a small slit in the side of each one so you can remove the inner membrane and all the seeds, so they are ready to be filled. Marinate the prepared chiles in the vodka for at least 12 hours before you prepare the filling.

To make the filling, melt the white or dark chocolate in the top of a double boiler over simmering water. Remove from the heat and mix in a shot of vodka and some freshly ground pepper. Fill the chiles using a pastry bag fitted with a small nozzle, or, if you don't have one, use a coffee spoon and a chopstick instead. Store the chiles in a container in the freezer until needed.

Sift confectioners' sugar over a serving plate. Grind some black pepper over the sugar.

To dip the chiles, melt the dark chocolate in the top of a double boiler over barely simmering water. Pour the melted chocolate into a glass and dip the chiles so that they are three-quarters coated in chocolate. Place them directly onto the serving plate to set before serving.

HINT: It is possible to blanch the de-seeded chiles to soften their flavor
or boil them for two minutes to remove most of their heat.

Once dried, the beans are hard and shrunken, having transformed from a white, purple, or pink color, depending on the variety, to a medium or dark brown.

The chocolate flavors are now in place, although they are not yet fully developed. The beans are ready to be shipped to the factory.

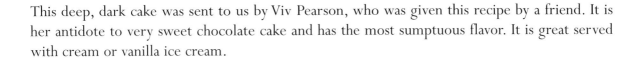

This deep, dark cake was sent to us by Viv Pearson, who was given this recipe by a friend. It is her antidote to very sweet chocolate cake and has the most sumptuous flavor. It is great served with cream or vanilla ice cream.

RICH STOUT

CAKE

Preparation time: 35 minutes
Cooking time: 1-1¹/₄ hours
Use: 9-inch-deep springform cake pan

1 cup (2 sticks) unsalted butter, softened

1³/₄ cups soft dark brown sugar

4 large eggs, beaten

1²/₃ cups all-purpose flour

¹/₂ teaspoon baking powder

2 teaspoons baking soda

1³/₄ cups Guinness or another stout
(let the head settle before using)

1 cup cocoa powder

5 ounces dark chocolate,
minimum 60% cocoa content, grated
(about 1¹/₂ cups)

Preheat the oven to 350°F.

Butter and line the cake pan with parchment paper. Alternatively, butter the pan and dust it with flour to coat, shaking out any excess.

In a large bowl, cream together the butter and sugar and gradually add the beaten eggs. In a another bowl, sift together the flour, baking powder, and baking soda. Mix together the Guinness and the cocoa in a large measuring cup or pitcher (you will need to persevere with mixing). Add the grated chocolate.

Add some of the flour to the cake batter, stir to combine, then add some stout and stir. Continue alternating with the flour and stout until all are used up and the batter is thoroughly mixed. The consistency will be quite soft.

Spoon into the pan and bake for one to one and a quarter hours or until a skewer inserted into the center of the cake comes out clean. You may need to cover the cake with foil after about an hour to prevent the top from browning.

Remove from the oven and let stand for 10 minutes before turning out onto a wire rack to cool.

HINT: Allow the head on the Guinness to settle before mixing in the cocoa.

Don't you dare tell your friends what's in this dish until they have eaten it. This recipe is a perfect example of why sweet and savory can be so successful together – partly because lamb is quite a sweet, rich meat which complements the chocolate perfectly. Annette Jones sent us this recipe. She was a runner-up in our Chocolate Recipe Competition in *Country Living* magazine, and describes it as a "wickedly decadent main course and a fragrant alternative to an ordinary casserole (stew)."

SWEDISH
CHOCOLATE COFFEE LAMB

Preparation time: 30 minutes
Cooking time: 1 hour
Serves: 4–6
Use: large, flameproof casserole dish, or other large flameproof and ovenproof pot

$^1/_3$ cup flour

$^1/_2$ teaspoon mustard powder

pinch of sea salt or kosher salt

freshly ground black pepper

$2^1/_4$ pounds very lean lamb (fillet or leg), cut into $1^1/_4$-inch cubes

$^1/_3$ cup ($^3/_4$ stick) unsalted butter

3 garlic cloves

1 large onion

12 shallots

1 tablespoon olive oil

1 tablespoon Kahlúa (or other coffee liqueur)

1 cup strong brewed coffee

4 cups good-quality lamb stock

2 ounces dark chocolate, minimum 60% cocoa content, broken into pieces

SPICES AND SEASONING

1 blade mace, crumbled

12 cardamom pods, crushed

1 vanilla bean, de-seeded

$^1/_2$ teaspoon nutmeg, grated

1 star anise

3 bay leaves, broken

FOR THE CROUTONS

1 slice white bread

1 slice whole wheat bread

olive oil

FOR GARNISHING

1 tablespoon crème fraîche or sour cream

handful chopped fresh parsley

Place all the spices and seasoning for the croutons in a heavy frying pan. Gently dry toast over very low heat for approximately 10 to 15 minutes, but do not let them burn. Tip into a small bowl and reserve until needed for the croutons. Preheat the oven to 425°F.

Season the flour with the mustard powder, salt, and pepper. Toss the lamb in the seasoned flour and coat well. Rub together two tablepoons of butter and the remaining seasoned flour.

HINT: Pour boiling water over the shallots and leave for 10 minutes to loosen their skins before peeling.

Crush the garlic, slice the onion into rings, and finely chop the shallots. Fry the garlic, onion, and shallots in the remaining butter and the olive oil until they are golden. Remove from the pan with a slotted spoon and set aside.

In the same pan, fry the flour-coated lamb in batches until browned on all sides. Remove and put in a flameproof and ovenproof pot and add the fried garlic, onion and shallots. Do not wash out the frying pan!

Add the Kahlúa and the coffee to the sticky brown residue in the frying pan and, over medium heat, whisk together for about four minutes, scraping up all the bits from the bottom of the pan, to form a glossy smooth sauce; the sauce should be reduced by half. Add the lamb stock and the flour and butter mixture, continuing to stir. Bring to a boil and pour over the meat and onion mixture.

Cook in the middle of the oven for 15 minutes, then reduce the temperature to 325°F for another 45 minutes or until the lamb is tender. Insert a knife into the center of a chunk – the lamb should just slide off.

While the meat is cooking, prepare the croutons. Blend all the reserved spices to a crumbled mass, discarding the cardamom pods. Cut the bread into cubes and gently fry with the spices and olive oil, adding more oil as it is absorbed by the bread. Set aside.

Once tender, remove the lamb from the oven and stir in the pieces of chocolate, ensuring it is completely blended throughout the stew.

Garnish with a swirl of crème fraîche or sour cream, a sprinkling of fresh chopped parsley, and the croûtons.

Serve with boiled new potatoes or mashed potatoes and simple vegetables.

CREATE A STIR

A keen organic vegetable gardener, cook, and chocolate lover, Lindsey Barrow was one of the runners-up in our *Country Living* recipe competition. She devised this recipe "after being inundated with zucchinis from her organic garden." Lindsey often bakes this loaf for charity cake sales and, because of the unusual combination of ingredients, it always sells out.

CHOCOLATE
ZUCCHINI BREAD

Preparation time: 20 minutes
Cooking time: 55 minutes
Use: 2-pound loaf pan
Makes: 8–10 slices

CAKE

6 ounces dark chocolate,
minimum 60% cocoa content, broken into pieces

8 ounces zucchini (about one 8-inch zucchini)

1¹/₂ cups all-purpose flour

1 teaspoon baking powder

1 teaspoon baking soda

1 teaspoon ground cinnamon

¹/₂ cup sugar

³/₄ cup sunflower oil

2 medium eggs

FROSTING

³/₄ cup (¹/₂ stick) unsalted butter, softened

3 cups confectioners' sugar

¹/₂ cup cocoa powder

water or liqueur (optional)

Preheat the oven to 350°F.

Brush the pan with a little oil and line the bottom with parchment paper if you have some at hand.

Melt the chocolate in the top of a double boiler over barely simmering water. Stir until smooth and keep warm.

Finely grate the zucchini.

Sift the flour, baking powder, baking soda, and cinnamon into a large bowl and mix in the sugar and grated zucchini.

In another bowl, beat together the oil and eggs. Pour into the flour mixture, stir, then stir in the melted chocolate.

Pour the batter into the prepared loaf pan and bake for 55 to 65 minutes, or until the loaf is well risen and a skewer inserted into the center comes out clean.

The freshly baked loaf is very fragile so let it cool in the pan for at least 15 minutes or until lukewarm, before turning it out carefully onto a wire rack to cool completely.

To make the frosting, cream the butter until light and fluffy. Sift together the confectioners' sugar and the cocoa powder, then beat into the creamed butter with enough liqueur or water to make a frosting that is easy to spread.

HINT: This loaf freezes well. Wrap it in foil and place it in a plastic bag before freezing.

Marian Ash created this quintessentially South American dish when she was reading *Like Water for Chocolate* by Laura Esquivel and then had a chat with a friend about the magical effect of chocolate on savory food. She began experimenting and came up with this recipe, which she suggests serving with corn tortillas and an avocado salad.

CHICKEN

MOLE

Preparation time: 20 minutes
Cooking time: 1½ hours
Use: large, flameproof casserole dish or another flameproof and ovenproof pot
Serves: 4

2 garlic cloves

2 large onions

2 smoked, dried Jalapeño chile peppers,
soaked and chopped, soaking water reserved,
or 2 teaspoons of smoked sweet paprika

8 chicken pieces on the bone

2 tablespoons olive oil

one 15-oz. can red kidney beans

one 14½-oz. can chopped tomatoes

2½ ounces dark chocolate,
minimum 60% cocoa content, broken into pieces

salt

Preheat the oven to 300°F.

Crush the garlic cloves and slice the onions.

Remove the seeds and chop the soaked chile peppers, and reserve the soaking water.

In a large, flameproof and ovenproof pot, heat a little olive oil and sear the chicken pieces in it. Brown lightly and then add the garlic and sliced onions.

Once the onions are lightly browned, add the tomatoes and the red kidney beans including their juice, the chopped chiles, their soaking juice, and two-thirds of the chocolate.

Bring to a simmer, then place in the oven and cook for at least one and a half hours.

Skim the surface to remove the fat from the chicken.

Taste, and adjust the seasoning with salt if necessary.

Add the rest of the dark chocolate to taste.

The sauce will be a rich, thick, velvety brown with a gloss all of its own.

HINT: Omit the chicken and double the quantity of beans for a vegetarian mole.

You don't need a sausage machine to make these heavenly sausages, but you will need a butcher who can sell you some organic pork sausage casings. Zena Leech-Calton entered our National Trust competition and this recipe leapt out at us as we trawled through all the entries. Testing and tasting the sausages was an adventure, but filling the sausage casings manually proved to be much easier than we had imagined it would be.

SPICY ORGANIC PORK & HERB
CHILEAN CHOCOLATE SAUSAGES

Preparation time: 30 minutes
Resting time: overnight
Cooking: 10–15 minutes
Makes: 16 small sausages or 10 large ones
Use: sausage machine or large pastry bag, with the $3/4$– to 1-inch nozzle

enough sausage casings for $2^1/4$ pounds mix

1 tablespoon vinegar

$1^1/4$ pounds organic belly of pork, coarsely ground

$1/2$ pound organic belly of pork, diced small

2 sage leaves, chopped

1 teaspoon chopped cilantro and stalks

1 teaspoon chopped flat-leaf parsley leaves

1 teaspoon chopped lemon thyme

2 tablespoons unsalted butter

1 tablespoon corn oil

6 ounces red onion, finely chopped

1 green chile, seeded and finely chopped

$1/2$-inch ginger root, peeled and finely chopped

2 garlic cloves, crushed

$1/2$ teaspoon ground mace

$1/2$ teaspoon ground paprika

$1/4$ teaspoon freshly grated nutmeg

$1/4$ teaspoon ground cumin

one $3^1/2$-oz. bar dark chocolate, minimum 60% cocoa content, broken into pieces

salt and freshly ground black pepper

Soak the sausage casings in a bowl of tepid water along with a tablespoon of vinegar for 30 minutes. They will become soft and elastic. Wash the casings thoroughly in cold water then run water through them by attaching them to the faucet.

Mix the ground and diced pork, sage, coriander, parsley, and lemon thyme in a bowl using your hands.

Heat the butter and oil in a frying pan and sauté the red onion, chile, ginger, and garlic until soft, but not browned. Add the mace, paprika, nutmeg, and cumin to the sautéed mixture while it is still hot. Cook together for a few minutes to release the flavor of the spices.

Melt the chocolate in the top of a double boiler over barely simmering water.

Add the onion and spice mixture and the melted chocolate to the bowl of pork and mix together well, seasoning with a good dash of salt and pepper.

Cover the bowl and leave in the fridge overnight.

Load up your sausage machine or pastry bag with the filling (if using a pastry bag, do not put all the filling into the pastry bag at once as it makes it more difficult to force it through). Ease the casing over the nozzle, tying the casing at the open end and leaving about three inches hanging loose from the knot. Feed the filling through to make one long, fat sausage, then, once the casing is almost full, tie a knot at the top end. Divide it into individual sausages by twisting each section in alternate directions to prevent the sausages unwinding. Cut the sausages in the middle of each twisted section.

Blanch the sausages in boiling, salted water for one minute before broiling or barbecuing them. Turn them frequently and try not to overcook them.

These sausages are delicious served with steamed brown rice flavored with ginger, and a two-bean salsa salad made with black beans, cannellini beans, olive oil, tomatoes, avocados, cilantro, garlic, peppers, onions, and seasoning.

This recipe must be made by hand to get the right texture. Roger Slater has a large airy kitchen so he proves his bread in a preheated oven before turning the oven on again to bake it. He suggests toasting the bread and eating it on its own or with a seafood appetizer such as smoked salmon.

CHOCOLATE, CHILE, & LIME
BREAD

Preparation time: 40 minutes
Rising time: 35 minutes
Cooking time: 20–25 minutes
Use: 2-pound loaf pan

$3/4$ ounces active dried yeast

2 tablespoons brown sugar

about $1^3/4$ cups warm water

about $3^1/2$ cups white bread flour

1 teaspoon salt

$4^1/2$ ounces dark chocolate,
minimum 60% cocoa content, chopped

1 lime, plus the juice from $1/2$ lime

1 dried red chile, seeded and finely chopped

$1/4$ cup olive oil

Mix together the yeast, sugar, and half the warm water to activate the yeast. Set aside in a warm place for about 15 minutes.

Sift the flour and salt into a mixing bowl, add the chopped chocolate, and the juice from the half-lime. Grate the peel of the whole lime and add the zest to the bowl. Thinly slice the lime, peel and all. Add half the sliced lime to the bowl and discard the rest. Add the chopped dried chile and the olive oil to the bowl, and mix roughly.

Once the yeast has become activated and frothed up, add it to the mixture and mix thoroughly by hand.

As the liquid is absorbed, add another quarter-cup of the warm water and continue to mix. When a dough ball starts to form, use your judgement to add as much of the remaining warm water as needed. The dough should be moist but not wet. If the dough becomes too wet, sprinkle in some extra flour to absorb the excess moisture. Continue to work the dough for 15 minutes.

Place the dough on a floured baking tray. Cover with a clean damp dishcloth and leave in a warm place for at least 20 minutes to rise.

Preheat the oven to 350°F.

Lightly oil the loaf pan with olive oil and put the dough in it, pressing down and shaping, not too firmly, then turn off the oven and place the pan in the warmed oven to stand for another 15 minutes.

Then turn the oven back on again, this time to 425°F, and bake for 20 minutes.

After 20 minutes, turn the bread out of the pan and tap the bottom with a wooden spoon – it should sound hollow. If it does, place the loaf on a wire rack to cool; if it doesn't, return to the oven (without the pan) for another five minutes.

HINT: For dough to rise, it needs moisture and warmth and no drafts.
If the air temperature is too low, the yeast will be slow to react; too high and it will die.

One Christmas, Margaret Ruhl created this recipe as a surprise for her husband who is a connoisseur of chocolate-coated ginger. It tastes and looks fantastic with spikes of ginger rising up out of the icing and is an absolute must for any ginger and chocolate fiend.

CHOCOLATE

GINGER CAKE

Preparation time: 15 minutes
Cooking time: 1 hour
Use: 7- or 8-inch round cake pan

CAKE

$^2/_3$ cup sugar

$^2/_3$ cup (1$^1/_4$ sticks) unsalted butter

3 large eggs

3 tablespoons of syrup from a jar of preserved ginger

1 cup self-rising flour

$^1/_3$ cup cocoa powder

3$^1/_2$ ounces preserved stem ginger, finely chopped (about $^1/_3$ cup)

ICING

3$^1/_2$ ounces crystallized ginger (about $^1/_2$ cup)

one 3$^1/_2$-oz. bar dark chocolate,
minimum 60% cocoa content, broken into pieces

To make the cake, preheat the oven to 350°F. Line the bottom of the cake pan with parchment paper. Alternatively, butter the pan and dust with flour to coat, tipping out any excess flour. Cream the sugar and butter until light and fluffy. Add the eggs, one at a time, beating well after each addition, then add the preserved ginger syrup, and lightly beat again. Sift the flour and cocoa, fold them into the mixture, then fold in the finely chopped preserved ginger.

Pour into the cake pan and bake for one hour or until a skewer inserted into the center comes out clean. Remove from the oven and leave in the pan for 10 minutes before turning out onto a wire rack, leaving the paper on. Let cool before making the icing.

To make the icing, finely chop the ginger. Melt the chocolate in the top of a double boiler over barely simmering water. Add the ginger and stir well. Once the cake has cooled, pour the icing over the cake using a butter knife or pastry spatula to spread it.

HINT: This cake is just as delicious with melted Maya Gold Chocolate poured over it.

TREASURES

Traces of caffeine and theobromine were discovered in 2002 in the remains of a brew found in cooking pots in north Belize. The pots came from a Maya burial site *c.*600 B.C. and showed that chocolate was used for food 1,000 years earlier than previously thought and that it was the Maya, not the Aztecs, who were the first to make a drink from it

TREASURES

Martine Hilton's mother grew up on the plantations of Sumatra and Java surrounded by cacao pods. Her father, who had trained as a chemist, devised a method of roasting the beans and then hand-grinding them to make bars of rich, fatty chocolate. This is a family recipe based upon ingredients that were available to her grandparents such as fresh coconut, cans of condensed milk, and her grandmother's favorite, hot ginger. Martine says it was often served when the ladies changed from sarongs into sweltering European dress after lunch to receive visitors. She has adapted this recipe and serves these squares at Christmas with Javanese coffee.

JAVANESE
GINGER SQUARES

Preparation time: 15 minutes
Chilling time: overnight
Use: 7 x 11-inch baking tray
Makes: about 25

four 3$^1/_2$-oz. bars dark chocolate,
minimum 60% cocoa content, broken into pieces

$^1/_2$ cup (1 stick) unsalted butter

one 14-oz. can condensed milk

9 ounces gingersnaps, crushed (about 2$^1/_2$ cups)

9 ounces crystallized ginger (about 2–2$^1/_2$ cups)

3 ounces flaked coconut (about 1 cup)

Melt the chocolate in the top of a double boiler over barely simmering water. Stir in the butter and condensed milk.

Crush the gingersnaps roughly in a plastic bag using a rolling pin. Chop the ginger into small pieces and set about a quarter of them aside. Into the chocolate mixture, stir the gingersnaps, three-quarters of the ginger, and the flaked coconut.

Spoon the mixture into the pan lined with waxed paper which comes up the sides of the pan and level the surface. Dot the surface with the reserved pieces of ginger.

Chill overnight in the pan. Lift out, using the paper to lift it, and cut into small squares.

HINT: Flaked coconut can be found in food stores and specialty food stores.

Florentines are another of those tempting treats that one eyes in pâtisserie windows, never imagining they could be within reach of the home cook. They are, in fact, not nearly as complicated as they look.

FLORENTINES

Preparation time: 20 minutes
Cooking time: 10–12 minutes
Cooling and decorating time: 25 minutes
Use: 2³/₄-inch cookie cutter, 2 baking sheets, preferably non-stick with little bumps
Makes: about 24

¹/₄ cup (¹/₂ stick) unsalted butter

¹/₂ cup heavy cream

¹/₂ cup sugar

¹/₄ cup glacé cherries, rinsed in hot water, drained, and cut into quarters

1 cup blanched almonds, finely chopped

¹/₂ cup slivered almonds

³/₄ cup candied orange peel, finely chopped

¹/₃ cup all-purpose flour

9 ounces dark chocolate, minimum 60% cocoa content, broken into pieces

Preheat the oven to 350°F. Butter and lightly flour the baking sheets.

Melt the butter along with the cream and sugar and bring slowly to a boil. Remove from the heat and stir in the cherries, the chopped and slivered almonds, and the candied peel, and sift in the flour.

Drop a teaspoonful of the mixture onto the baking sheets, leaving plenty of room between — they will double in size as they bake, and flatten each one with a fork dipped in cold water.

Bake for five to six minutes, remove from the oven, and coax each into a circular shape by placing the cookie cutter over it. Return to the oven and bake for another five to six minutes, until lightly browned at the edges. Remove from the oven and let them set for a few minutes on the baking sheets, then use a spatula to transfer them to a rack to cool.

Melt the chocolate in the top of a double boiler over barely simmering water. Spread the smooth undersides of the florentines with chocolate using a butter knife or pastry spatula. When it is on the point of setting, create wavy lines across the chocolate by dragging a serrated knife from side to side across the chocolate. Let them set.

HINT: This recipe is also delicious using milk, white, or Maya Gold Chocolate.

A brazil nut has the calorie content of half an egg and is especially rich in amino acids so you may feel a mixture of guilt and contentment as you tuck into these delicious cookies. This recipe was sent to us by Lorna Dowell, another of our National Trust chocolate competition finalists. Lorna was inspired to experiment after a delicious tea at the National Trust site at Dapdune Wharf, England, where she ate soft-baked chocolate chip cookies.

CHOCOLATE BRAZIL
SOFT-BAKED COOKIES

Preparation time: 15 minutes
Cooking time: 20 minutes
Use: 2$\frac{1}{2}$-inch cookie cutter, cookie sheet
Makes: 20

$\frac{1}{3}$ cup ($\frac{3}{4}$ stick) unsalted butter

$\frac{1}{4}$ cup sugar

1 large egg, beaten

1$\frac{1}{3}$ cups whole wheat flour

1$\frac{1}{2}$ teaspoons baking powder

$\frac{1}{2}$ teaspoon vanilla extract

1–2 tablespoons milk

3 ounces dark chocolate,
minimum 60% cocoa content, roughly chopped

3 ounces milk chocolate,
preferably 34% cocoa content, roughly chopped

2 ounces brazil nuts, chopped (about $\frac{1}{2}$ cup)

$\frac{1}{2}$ teaspoon salt

Preheat the oven to 350°F. Grease a cookie sheet with melted butter.

Cream the butter and sugar in a bowl until light and fluffy. Beat in the egg. Sift the flour and baking powder once, returning the bran to the sifted flour, then fold it into the mixture. The bran gives a distinctive flavor and texture to the cookies. Beat well, adding the vanilla extract and enough milk to make a pliable dough. Mix it with your hands, adding the milk in stages until the dough is fairly soft, but not sticky. Add the chopped chocolate, nuts, and salt, and distribute evenly through the dough. Roll out onto a lightly floured board to a thickness of about a quarter-inch. Press out the cookies using the cookie cutter and place them on the greased cookie sheet, leaving plenty of room in between cookies.

Bake in the center of the oven for about 20 minutes. Watch them carefully so they don't overcook. Remove from the oven and let cool on the cookie sheet for a few minutes before transferring to a wire rack to cool completely.

HINT: All flour should be sifted before you use it. Sifting flour is important, not just to remove any little foreign bodies that may be in the flour, but also to aerate it.

Gingerbread was made with spices, ginger, and honey in medieval times, but in the seventeenth century, the honey was replaced by treacle. Teresa Jackson makes this chocolate recipe for the Halloween Carnival that takes place in Belfast each year. She has been spreading the word about real chocolate and Fairtrade at work and has been a great fan of Green & Black's for many years.

CHOCOLATE SPICE
GINGERBREAD

Preparation time: 40 minutes
Cooking time: 50 minutes
Use: 7-inch square cake pan, 3 inches deep
Makes: 8 slices

$^1/_2$ cup (1 stick) unsalted butter

2 ounces Maya Gold or other good-quality, dark, orange-flavored chocolate, broken into pieces

2 ounces dark chocolate, minimum 60% cocoa content, broken into pieces

$^1/_3$ cup dark brown sugar

$^1/_4$ cup treacle (if unavailable, use molasses)

$^2/_3$ cup buttermilk

$^3/_4$ cup ready-to-eat prunes

$1^1/_3$ cups all-purpose flour

1 teaspoon baking soda

2 teaspoons ground ginger

1 teaspoon cinnamon

1 large egg, lightly beaten

Preheat the oven to 325°F. Line the pan with parchment paper.

Cut the butter into cubes and place in a heavy saucepan along with the two chocolates, sugar, treacle, and buttermilk. Heat gently until the ingredients have melted, then set aside to cool.

Snip the prunes into small pieces with kitchen scissors. Sift the flour into a large bowl along with the baking soda and spices. Pour the chocolate mixture into the bowl and beat thoroughly with a wooden spoon, then add the beaten egg and beat again. Fold in the prunes.

Pour the mixture into the prepared pan and level off the surface using a butter knife or pastry spatula. Bake for about 50 minutes. Remove from the oven and let cool in the pan for about 10 minutes. Turn out onto a wire rack and let cool completely. Wrap in waxed paper and store in an airtight container.

HINT: This cake is wonderfully moist and will keep for a week in an airtight container. It is best eaten the day after it is made.

Dr Barry Alcock, a runner-up in our National Trust Chocolate Recipe Competition, sent us this regional French recipe which originates in St. Pourçain on the upper Loire. He points out that "these feather-light cakes have a name for which there is no polite translation. They are simply 'Nun's Farts.' "

PETS

DE NONNE

Preparation time: 20 minutes
Cooking time: 4 hours or overnight
Makes: 50
Use: 2 non-stick baking sheets

5 ounces dark chocolate,
minimum 60% cocoa content, roughly chopped

3 large egg whites

salt

1/2 cup sugar

1 cup walnuts, roughly chopped

1 ounce angelica, diced

2 teaspoons dark rum

Preheat the oven to 350°F. If you don't have non-stick baking sheets, line ordinary ones with foil.

Place the roughly chopped chocolate in the fridge for about one hour.

Beat the egg whites with a pinch of salt until stiff peaks form. Beat in the sugar, a little at a time, until the mixture becomes glossy. Fold in the nuts, chocolate, and angelica, and then fold in the rum.

Place heaped teaspoons of the mixture on the baking sheets, leaving plenty of room in between.

Bake in the oven for five minutes and then turn off the oven and leave them for about four hours or overnight.

Store the cakes in an airtight container.

HINT: Be careful not to overbeat the egg whites. They should form stiff, shiny peaks, but if they start to separate and resemble snow, you have gone too far.

Roger Moore sent in this recipe with a note saying "My late mother-in-law was an accomplished cook, whose cakes and puddings were irresistible to potential sons-in-law. The origins of her recipes lay in a motley collection of old, well-thumbed cookery books, though most had been adapted using the personal touch, as they became family traditions. The Chocolate Apple Cake has always been my favorite and seems to improve over time, if any is left over for tomorrow!"

MY MOTHER-IN-LAW'S

CHOCOLATE APPLE CAKE

Preparation time: 30 minutes
Cooking time: 50–55 minutes
Use: 8^1/$_2$-inch round cake pan
Serves: 8

CAKE

1 cup hazelnuts

1^1/$_4$ cups (2^1/$_2$ sticks) unsalted butter

^{3}/$_4$ cup sugar

3 large eggs

2 cups self-rising flour

1 teaspoon baking powder

about ^{1}/$_4$ cup strong brewed coffee

2 ounces dark chocolate,
minimum 60% cocoa content, coarsely grated

FILLING

1^1/$_2$ pounds Bramley apples (if unavailable, use tart cooking apples)

1 large lemon

1^1/$_2$ tablespoons rhubarb jam or fruit compôte

ICING

two 3^1/$_2$-oz. bars dark chocolate,
minimum 60% cocoa content, broken into pieces

two tablespoons unsalted butter

2 drops vanilla extract

1 teaspoon strong brewed coffee

Preheat the oven to 350°F. Butter and flour the cake pan.

To make the cake, crush the hazelnuts, not too finely, and dry-toast them in a frying pan until they are golden. They burn very easily so keep a close eye on them. Cream the butter and sugar together. Whisk the eggs and add to the creamed mixture along with a little of the flour. Mix together well. Sift in the remaining flour, the baking powder, and enough coffee to make a soft mix. Set aside a quarter of the grilled hazelnuts, then fold the rest into the batter, along with the coarsely grated chocolate.

Pour the batter into the cake pan. Bake for 50 to 55 minutes. Let the cake cool a little in the pan, before turning out to cool completely on a wire rack.

Meanwhile, prepare the filling. Peel and roughly chop the apples. Place in a saucepan along with the grated rind and juice of the lemon, and the jam. Cover and cook over low heat, stirring occasionally, until the apple pieces are soft, but not mushy.

Once the cake has cooled, carefully cut it in half horizontally and fill with the cooled apple mixture.

To make the icing, melt the chocolate along with the coffee in the top of a double boiler over barely simmering water. Remove from the heat and stir in the butter and vanilla extract. Let cool a little before pouring over the cake, allowing the icing to run gently over the sides.

Decorate with the reserved hazelnuts.

HINT: This cake can be made with almost any nuts,
especially pine nuts or almonds, which do not have to be grilled.

Once they arrive at the chocolate factory, the beans are pitted and cleaned. A brief, intense blast of heat is fired at them to loosen the shells from the nibs that nestle inside. Crushers, sieves, and streams of air are then used to force open the shells and release the nibs.

Philippa Jacobs lived in Cape Town for three years and this is her favorite South African recipe. It always reminds her of the very wet Cape winters when a walk with her dogs on the slopes of Table Mountain in the rain and wind was followed by a traditional Sunday roast and Tipsy Tart. Her variation on the recipe includes a covering of grated dark chocolate.

CAPE GINGER
TIPSY TART

Preparation time: 40 minutes
Baking time: 35 minutes
Use: 9-inch tart pan or a pie dish of a size suitable for serving

BATTER

1 teaspoon baking soda

8 ounces pitted dates, chopped (about $1^1/_4$–$1^1/_2$ cups)

$^1/_2$ cup boiling water

3 tablespoons unsalted butter

$^3/_4$ cup granulated sugar

2 large eggs

2 cups flour

1 teaspoon baking powder

pinch of salt

1 ounce preserved ginger, chopped

4 ounces glacé or dried cherries, chopped

$^1/_2$ cup walnuts, chopped

half of a $3^1/_2$-oz. bar dark chocolate, minimum 60% cocoa content

SYRUP

$^1/_3$ cup granulated sugar

1 cup minus 2 tablespoons water

salt

1 teaspoon vanilla extract

2 tablespoons unsalted butter

$^1/_4$ cup brandy or dark rum

heavy cream or vanilla ice cream for serving

Preheat the oven to 350°F. Grease the dish well with butter.

Put the dates in a bowl, pat them with the baking soda, and pour the boiling water over them. Stir and let cool.

Cream the butter and sugar, add the eggs, and beat thoroughly. Sift together the flour, baking powder, and salt, and stir into the creamed batter.

Add the date mixture, ginger, cherries, and walnuts.

Spoon the mixture into the pie dish and bake for 35 minutes. Place the chocolate in the freezer.

Prepare the syrup so you can pour it over the tart the minute it comes out of the oven. Boil all the ingredients for the syrup together for about six minutes until they form a syrup.

Remove the tart from the oven and prick the surface all over with a fork. Immediately pour the hot syrup over it, then grate the chilled chocolate over the top before serving with a dollop of cream.

HINT: If you prefer, you can use pecans instead of walnuts.

Strictly, these aren't really tuiles as the original golden "tuiles" are named after the tiles that dominate the rooftops of Provence, and, although these Chocolate Tuiles still bear the curved shape, their color has changed. They are the perfect accompaniment to ice cream or a chocolate mousse.

CHOCOLATE
TUILES

Preparation time: 10 minutes
Chilling time: 1 hour
Cooking time: 15 minutes
Use: non-stick baking sheet, preferably one with little round bumps all over it
Makes: 12

1 large egg

1 large egg white

$^1/_2$ cup confectioners' sugar

3 tablespoons all-purpose flour

2 tablespoons cocoa powder

1 teaspoon heavy cream

2 tablespoons unsalted butter, melted and cooled

1 cup pine nuts and slivered hazelnuts

Whisk together the egg and the egg white in a bowl. Add the confectioners' sugar, flour, cocoa, cream, and melted butter in that order and mix until smooth. Stir in the pine nuts and slivered hazelnuts.

Place heaped tablespoons of the mixture onto the non-stick trays, leaving plenty of room in between, and refrigerate for one hour.

Preheat the oven to 350°F.

Dip a fork in warm water and, shaking off any excess water, flatten the mixture into discs using the back of the fork.

Bake for 10 minutes or until the "tuiles" are firm and have an even color. Remove from the oven and immediately place them over a rolling pin to give them a curved shape. Let cool and store in an airtight container.

HINT: The "tuiles" look wonderful served upside down, overlapping one another in rows in the same way as they would be laid on a roof in the south of France.

If you need to make this recipe for more than six people, double the quantities but use two separate pans – it begins to look like a great beast if you make one enormous one! This healthier version of a meringue roulade which uses yogurt instead of cream is delicious with almost any fruit but looks especially effective if you use green and red grapes or any berries.

MERINGUE ROULADE
WITH CHOCOLATE

Preparation time: 30 minutes
Cooking time: 45 minutes
Use: 15 x 11-inch baking tray
Serves: 6–8

ROULADE

4 large egg whites

1 cup superfine sugar

2–3 tablespoons confectioners' sugar for dusting

2 tablespoons cocoa powder for dusting

2$^1/_4$ cups whole milk yogurt

one 3$^1/_2$-oz. bar dark chocolate, minimum 60% cocoa content, chopped into small chunks

11 ounces raspberries (about 2 cups)

RASPBERRY COULIS

8 ounces raspberries (about 1$^1/_2$ cups)

$^1/_3$ cup confectioners' sugar

Cut out two sheets of parchment paper so that the sides rise about two inches from the bottom of the baking sheet. Butter the baking sheet, and then line it with one piece of the parchment paper. Reserve the other piece.

Preheat the oven to 200°F.

Beat the egg whites until soft peaks form. Continue to beat, gradually adding half the sugar. Continue to beat until the mixture is stiff but not dry. Fold in the remaining sugar.

Spoon the meringue into the prepared paper-lined pan, spreading it evenly into the corners. Bake in the preheated oven for 40 to 45 minutes, until it is lightly colored and firm yet spongy when pressed. Let cool for about one hour.

To make the coulis, purée the raspberries in a blender and then strain them into a bowl. Stir in the confectioners' sugar to taste.

Place a large sheet of parchment paper on the counter and dust with the confectioners' sugar and the cocoa. Turn the baked meringue (still in its paper) upside down onto the large sheet so that what was the top of the meringue is now on the sugar and cocoa, and is now the bottom. Carefully peel away the paper.

Spread the yogurt over the meringue. Scatter the chocolate chunks evenly over the yogurt and then scatter the raspberries evenly on top. Very carefully roll up the roulade using the paper as a support. Save any leftover sugar and cocoa for sprinkling over the roulade before serving. Chill in the fridge until needed, but for no more than five hours. Serve with the raspberry coulis.

HINT: Do not worry about the meringue cracking slightly as you roll it up — it will look beautiful once you have sprinkled the leftover confectioners' sugar and cocoa over it.

Jo Gilks gave up her lucrative job in the City of London for food. She has always loved to cook and has forged a very different, yet often equally stressful, career for herself as a chef. Her Chocolate Pecan Pie has become a Thanksgiving dinner favorite and she warns you not to be put off by the crumbly texture of the pastry dough – it is difficult to roll but worth the trouble.

JO'S CHOCOLATE

PECAN PIE

Preparation time: 35 minutes plus 25 minutes chilling
Cooking time: 1 hour, 25 minutes
Use: 11-inch removable-bottomed fluted tart pan
Serves 8–10

PASTRY DOUGH

2 cups all-purpose flour

2/3 cup confectioners' sugar

2/3 cup (1 1/4 sticks) unsalted butter, cold

2 large egg yolks

FILLING

10 ounces dark chocolate,
minimum 60% cocoa content, broken into pieces

2 cups shelled pecans, chopped

3 large eggs, beaten

1 packed cup light soft brown sugar

1 cup evaporated milk

1 teaspoon vanilla extract

1/4 cup (1/2 stick) unsalted butter, melted

To make the dough, sift together the flour and confectioners' sugar and cut the butter into cubes.

Place in a food processor and mix together, adding the egg yolks at the end to form a dough.

Carefully roll out the dough. You will need quite a lot of flour on your board and rolling pin as it sticks easily. The pastry dough needs to be very thin. Lift it carefully into the tart pan by rolling it up on the rolling pin, then slowly unroll it over the pan, press into the bottom and sides, and trim away the excess, but allow a little extra as the crust will shrink slightly. Chill in the fridge for about 30 minutes. Preheat the oven to 350°F.

Bake the pie shell blind by lining it with parchment paper or foil, filled with dried beans, and baked for about 15 minutes.

Remove the beans and paper and return the pie crust to the oven for another 10 minutes or until it is lightly colored. Remove from the oven and set aside while you make the filling. Reduce the oven temperature to 325°F.

Melt the chocolate in the top of a double boiler over barely simmering water. Mix together all the remaining ingredients for the filling, then stir in the melted chocolate. Spoon into the pie shell and return it to the oven for about one hour. Watch the crust carefully and if necessary, cover with foil to prevent it burning.

HINT: Any dried beans or legumes can be used for blind baking – red, kidney, or black beans, corn or rice – all they are doing is putting weight on the pie crust so that it doesn't rise during baking. Once cooled, they can be used again and again.

MYSTICAL

Hurricane Iris devastated Belize on October 21st 2001. It destroyed many homes and crops and caused havoc for the cacao that survived, but more cacao trees have since been replanted by the growers. This cacao pod has been bored into by a woodpecker.

The drama of a soufflé straight from the oven will always stir a table of dinner party guests. Remember the success of a soufflé is in the rising, so take note of the hints at the bottom of the page. This is another of our trusted tester, Jo Gilks's, foolproof recipes.

CHOCOLATE SOUFFLÉ
WITH CARAMEL SAUCE

Preparation time: 20 minutes
Cooking time: 10-15 minutes
Use: six 2^1/$_2$-inch ramekins or custard cups
Serves: 6

1 teaspoon unsalted butter

1 tablespoon sugar

1 tablespoon cocoa powder

SOUFFLE

4 ounces dark chocolate,
minimum 60% cocoa content, broken into pieces

^{3}/$_4$ cup cocoa powder

8 egg whites

^{1}/$_4$ cup superfine sugar

CARAMEL SAUCE

one 3^1/$_2$-oz. bar caramel-filled chocolate, broken into pieces

1 tablespoon heavy cream

Preheat the oven to 375°F.

To prepare the ramekins, melt the butter and brush the insides of the ramekins. Mix the sugar with the cocoa and sprinkle into each ramekin until coated, shaking out any excess. Set aside.

Melt the chocolate in the top of a double boiler over barely simmering water.

Mix the cocoa with two-thirds cup of cold water in a saucepan, then bring to a boil whisking continuously. Boil for 10 seconds. Transfer the cocoa mixture to a large mixing bowl and mix with the melted chocolate.

Prepare the Caramel Sauce so that it will be ready when you serve the soufflé. Place the caramel-chocolate and the cream in the top of a double boiler over barely simmering water. Stir before serving.

Continue with the soufflés by beating the egg whites in a large bowl until soft peaks form. Add the sugar and continue beating until stiff peaks form. Add one-quarter of the beaten whites to the cocoa mixture and whisk until thoroughly blended. Gently fold in the remaining egg whites using a metal spoon to cut through the whites as you fold so that you do not knock the air out of it.

Fill each prepared ramekin to the rim with the soufflé mixture and, using a butter knife, level off the surface. Run your thumb around the rim of each ramekin, pushing away the soufflé mixture, so that it does not stick to the edge and will rise evenly.

Bake the soufflés for about 10 to 15 minutes. Remove from the oven and pour a little Caramel Sauce over each soufflé and serve immediately.

HINT: When brushing the ramekins with the melted butter, brush from the bottom of the ramekin up towards the rim – this seems to help the soufflé to rise evenly. Remember not to open the oven door while the soufflé is cooking or the rush of cold air may prevent it from rising as high as you would wish.

Not such a predictable pudding after all, each of these mousses is a little different from the next one – sometimes it's the texture and with others a surprise flavor. Only the Chocolate and Lemongrass Mousse will take more than 25 minutes to prepare and at the most they will take six hours to set.

EGGLESS
HILARY METH'S

Chill for a minimum of 2 hours. Serves 4–6

two 3$\frac{1}{2}$-oz. bars dark chocolate, minimum 60% cocoa content, broken into pieces

1$\frac{3}{4}$ cups canned coconut milk

2 gelatin leaves or $\frac{1}{2}$-package granulated gelatin

2 tablespoons confectioners' sugar

2 teaspoons vanilla extract

Melt the chocolate in the top of a double boiler over barely simmering water. In another pan, gently heat the coconut milk, add the gelatin, and stir until dissolved. Sift the confectioners' sugar and add to the coconut milk, stirring to dissolve. Finally, add the vanilla and the melted chocolate and whisk together. Dust with cocoa, and decorate with roasted coffee beans, coconut flakes, or toasted pine nuts.

LIGHT
AND DARK

Chill for a minimum of 1 hour. Serves 6

two 3$\frac{1}{2}$-oz. bars dark chocolate, minimum 60% cocoa content, finely chopped

$\frac{1}{4}$ cup whole milk

2 large egg yolks

$\frac{1}{2}$ teaspoon vanilla extract

4 large egg whites

3 tablespoons sugar

Melt the chocolate and the milk in the top of a double boiler over barely simmering water. Stir together and then set aside to cool slightly. Stir the egg yolks into the chocolate until well blended, then stir in the vanilla. In a large bowl, beat the egg whites until soft peaks form. Add the sugar gradually and continue to beat until stiff and glossy. Stir a ladleful of egg whites into the chocolate mixture to lighten it, then gently fold in the rest of the egg whites. Transfer the mixture into your chosen container and chill for at least an hour.

HINT: Always use eggs at room temperature. Do not overbeat egg whites and remember to use a clean bowl. Use the melted chocolate while it is still warm to the touch. Do not let the melted chocolate and egg yolk mixture cool down too much, otherwise it will be difficult to mix in the egg whites.

WHITE CHOCOLATE, CARDAMOM MOUSSE

NIGEL SLATER'S

Chill for 4 hours. Serves 6–8

8 plump green cardamom pods

1/2 cup milk

3 bay leaves

9 ounces good-quality white chocolate, broken into pieces (about 1 1/2 cups)

1 1/4 cups whipping cream

3 large egg whites

cocoa powder for dusting

Crack open the cardamom pods and extract the seeds. Crush them lightly and then put them, along with the milk and the bay leaves, in a small saucepan. Gently warm the milk until it is close to boiling point, then remove from the heat and set aside to infuse. Melt the chocolate in the top of a double boiler over barely simmering water. As soon as it starts to melt turn off the heat, leaving the top pan in place. Whip the cream to form soft mounds; it should not be stiff. In another bowl, beat the egg whites until stiff peaks form. When the chocolate has completely melted, remove from the heat and strain the spiced milk mixture into it. Mix the chocolate and milk together until velvety. Stir a spoonful of the egg whites into the chocolate mixture, then gently fold in the remaining egg whites using a large metal spoon. Gently fold in the softly whipped cream. Spoon into containers and refrigerate for four hours. Dust with cocoa just before serving.

DARK

WITH COFFEE

Chill for at least 6 hours. Serves 6

5 ounces dark chocolate,
minimum 60% cocoa content, broken into pieces

2 tablespoons brewed coffee

¼ cup (½ stick) plus 1 tablespoon unsalted butter

3 large eggs, separated

3 tablespoons sugar

cocoa powder

Melt the chocolate along with the coffee and butter in the top of a double boiler over barely simmering water. Remove from the heat and stir. Stir in the egg yolks until the mixture is very smooth. In a bowl, beat the egg whites until soft peaks form, add the sugar, and beat until the mixture is stiff and glossy. Fold a ladleful into the chocolate and then add the rest of the egg whites delicately, to retain as much air as possible and ensuring no white spots from the meringue remain. Spoon into a serving bowl or six individual ramekins and chill for at least six hours. Dust with cocoa powder before serving but do not return the mousse to the fridge at this stage as the cocoa will absorb moisture.

A French family gave Angela Dempsey this recipe in the Seventies. She has since added the black currants and honey which has confirmed its position as her family's favorite pudding.

BITTER CHOCOLATE MOUSSE
WITH BLACK CURRANTS

Chill for a minimum of 1 hour. Serves 4–6

$^1/_4$ cup of black currants topped and tailed or canned black currants, strained

2 teaspoons honey

5 ounces Hazelnut and Currant Dark Chocolate or other good-quality fruit and nut chocolate, broken into pieces (about 1 cup)

5 egg whites

2 tablespoons sugar

2 egg yolks

Over a gentle heat, let the black currants soften in the honey. Once softened, remove from the heat and let cool. Melt the chocolate in the top of a double boiler over barely simmering water and let cool slightly. In a large bowl, beat the egg whites until soft peaks form, then add the sugar. Continue to beat until stiff and glossy. Stir the egg yolks into the melted chocolate then mix in one-third of the egg whites. Gently fold in the remaining egg whites. Spoon the black currants into the bottoms of your containers, then pour in the chocolate mousse. Chill for at least one hour before serving.

SIMPLE WHITE

Chill for a minimum of 4 hours. Serves 4–6

four 3$^1/_2$-oz. bars good-quality white chocolate, broken into pieces (about 2–2$^1/_2$ cups)

3 gelatin leaves

3 cups whipping cream

5 large egg yolks

1 cup confectioners' sugar

3–4 tablespoons Grand Marnier

Melt the chocolate in the top of a double boiler over barely simmering water. Dissolve the gelatin in two tablespoons of warmed cream. Beat the egg yolks and sugar, add the Grand Marnier, gelatin cream, and melted chocolate, and stir together well. Whip the remaining cream until thick and then fold into the chocolate and egg yolk mixture. Pour into a mold or individual ramekins and chill for four hours. This mousse is delicious served with a raspberry coulis and visitandines or with a crust of melted dark chocolate, poured on top and left to harden.

HINT: Remember to use a metal spoon when folding in the egg whites and to cut through the mixture as you fold. This way you do not knock the air out of the beaten whites and the mousse remains light and fluffy.

Rachel Green runs her own business cooking for four to four hundred people. She has cooked many times for the Royal Family and was recently filmed by the BBC. It was at a demonstration in aid of the Bosnian Support Fund, a charity that supports the continuing needs of refugees in Bosnia, that we tried this recipe. A farmer's daughter from Lincolnshire, Rachel is dedicated to supporting and promoting regional producers.

CHOCOLATE AND LEMONGRASS
MOUSSE

Chilling time: 2 hours
Serves: 6

3 sticks of lemongrass

1 cup milk

10 ounces milk chocolate,
preferably 34% cocoa content, broken into pieces

1¹/₂ gelatin leaves or ¹/₂-package granulated gelatin

¹/₄ cup sugar

1¹/₄ cups heavy cream

Finely chop the lemongrass into small pieces or grind in a food processor or mortar and pestle. Pour the milk into a large, heavy saucepan, add the lemongrass, and bring to a boil. Remove from the heat and let infuse for one hour. Melt the chocolate in the top of a double boiler over barely simmering water. Whisk the sugar and gelatin into the milk and return to a low heat, stirring continuously until the gelatin has melted. Remove from the heat and stir in the melted chocolate. Let cool slightly. Strain the mixture to remove the lemongrass. Let cool down completely. Whip the cream in a bowl until it begins to thicken, but it should not be too stiff. Gently fold into the chocolate mixture. Spoon the mousse into your chosen containers.

HINT: Set the mousse first in a large bowl before transferring to individual containers, then using a tablespoon and a clean finger, you can mould the mousse into your desired shape before garnishing.

This is one of those recipes that people either love or hate. It is irresistible if you are addicted to Toblerone or like a sweet mousse, and is the ultimate test of whether you have a sweet tooth.

CHOCOLATE NOUGAT
MOUSSE

Chilling time: 6 hours
Serves: 6

10¹/₂ ounces Toblerone, broken into pieces, reserving one piece for decoration

6 tablespoons boiling water

1¹/₄ cups crème fraîche or sour cream

2 egg whites

Place the chocolate and the boiling water in the top of a double boiler over barely simmering water and let the chocolate melt slowly. Remove from the heat, cool until it thickens and then fold in the crème fraîche. In a bowl, beat the egg whites until stiff peaks form and fold into the mixture. Chill in the fridge for at least six hours.

Once removed from the bean, the nibs are then roasted at over 100°C (212°F) to develop the rich flavor and characteristic color of cocoa.

The roasted nibs are then ground to produce cocoa liquor (or cocoa mass) which is made up of cocoa particles suspended in 50 to 55 percent cocoa butter.

The cocoa liquor is then transformed into chocolate by further processing and the addition of other ingredients. It can also be separated into cocoa powder and liquid cocoa butter.

"Cocoa content" is the term used to describe the total amount of cocoa-derived material in a finished chocolate. The percentage of cocoa content declared on chocolate packaging can refer to a combination of cocoa liquor and extra cocoa butter, as in most chocolate bars, cocoa butter in white chocolate, or just cocoa liquor, but this is rarely used on its own.

Cocoa Butter

Cocoa Liquor

Cocoa Powder

Originally created by Eric Charot, whose London restaurant, Interlude de Charot, gained a Michelin star within eleven months of opening, this unusual take on soup was discovered when the New Covent Garden Soup Co. marketing team was out "researching" new recipes. Eating out was always one of the most enjoyable parts of their job and was considered to be a vital part of the creative process.

CHOCOLATE

SOUP

Preparation time: 30 minutes
Chilling time: 2 hours
Use: an electric beater
Serves: 6

3 cups milk

1 cup heavy cream

18 ounces dark chocolate,
minimum 60% cocoa content, coarsely chopped

$1/4$ cup sugar

1 tablespoon water

8 large egg yolks

1 cup whipping cream

6 tablespoons skinned hazelnuts

rind of 1 orange, finely grated

6 teaspoons Grand Marnier

Bring the milk and heavy cream to a boil and add the chocolate. Set aside.

Heat the sugar with the water to make a syrup. When the sugar has melted, bring to a boil and boil for one minute. Start to whisk the egg yolks, then gradually pour the syrup over the yolks, whisking continuously.

Once the sugar has been incorporated, continue to whisk until the mixture is cold. The mixture will double in volume. Whip the cream and fold it in.

Combine the egg mixture with the chocolate sauce. Distribute the mixture between the individual bowls.

Preheat the oven to 400°F.

Toast the hazelnuts on a tray in the oven. Watch them carefully after about seven minutes as they burn easily.

Chill the soup for at least two hours.

Coarsely chop the hazelnuts and then sprinkle the hazelnuts and the grated orange zest over the soup and drizzle sparingly with Grand Marnier before serving as an appetizer.

HINT: Instead of adding the Grand Marnier and hazelnuts on top of the soup,
try pouring a teaspoon of Grand Marnier in the bottom of the bowl, then some soup,
followed by a layer of nuts, and then the rest of the soup.

Inspired by the popularity of tarts, Isobel Wakemen transformed her reliable Chocolate and Seville Orange Mousse into this Moorish Tart, which brightens up the dark February days when Seville oranges, with their wizened and knarled skins and bitter flavor, are a truly seasonal treat.

MOORISH

TART

Preparation time: 30 minutes
Cooking time: 40 minutes
Chilling time: 3 hours
Use: 8-inch fluted tart pan

PASTRY DOUGH

1¹/₃ cups all-purpose flour

¹/₃ cup confectioners' sugar

¹/₂ cup (1 stick) plus 1 tablespoon unsalted butter

grated zest of 1 Seville orange
(reserve the orange for the filling)

1 large egg, beaten

FILLING

5 ounces dark chocolate,
minimum 60% cocoa content, broken into pieces

1 cup heavy cream

4 large egg yolks

¹/₄ cup light brown sugar

juice of 1 Seville orange

Preheat the oven to 375°F.

To make the dough, blend the flour, confectioners' sugar, butter, and orange zest in a food processor to the breadcrumb stage, or else rub the ingredients together between your fingers. Add the beaten egg and mix until the pastry forms a ball. Wrap in waxed paper and let rest in the fridge for 30 minutes.

Roll out the dough on a lightly floured board and place it in the tart pan. Prick the bottom with a fork and cover it with foil and baking beans, bake it blind for 20 minutes, then remove the beans and the foil and continue to bake for another 10 minutes. Remove from the oven and let cool.

Melt the chocolate with the cream in the top of a double boiler over barely simmering water, then remove the top pan from the heat.

To make the filling, beat the egg yolks and sugar until light and fluffy. Give the melted chocolate and cream a stir, then add the egg mixture to the chocolate. Set top pan back over the simmering water and stir until the mixture thickens. Add the orange juice and stir for about two to three minutes or until the mixture thickens again. Do not let the mixture boil. Pour into the cooled pie shell and chill until set.

HINT: Seville oranges freeze well, so if using right from the freezer,
grate the zest before thawing.

KUKUH

OR XOCOLATL

Theobroma, the genus that all cacao trees belong to, literally means "food of the gods" from the Greek *theos* for "god" and *broma*, meaning "food or drink." The Swedish naturalist Carolus Linnaeus named the tree in the eighteenth century in tribute to the Maya and Aztec drink.

In Mexico, cocoa beans served as currency and the "food of the gods" was also at the heart of many rituals and ceremonies. This heady, aromatic, cocoa beverage, *xocolatl* or *kukuh*, was favored by Montezuma, the sixteenth-century king of the Aztecs, who drank it as a potent aphrodisiac. A simple infusion, it is spiced with chile and thickened with ground corn.

On a recent trip to Belize, Cluny Brown, our marketing manager, was given a bowl of *kukuh* and was told how to make this refreshing, slightly watery drink. Cocoa beans are roasted on a *comal*, a smooth griddle, until their skins fall away, then they are ground together with a little corn and ground black pepper or dried, toasted chile pepper. A little sugar is usually added, although in ancient times the Maya used forest honey. The drink can be served hot, tepid, or cold, and given the extreme heat and humidity in Belize, it is delicious chilled and very different from the Western version we enjoy on cold winter days.

Auzibio Sho, who works at the Toledo Cocoa Growers Association in southern Belize, claims that not only is it good for general well-being, it is also great for inducing labor as well. *Kukuh* is also consumed for health and energy and is given to sick people and those who need to work hard.

To make this revitalizing drink yourself, take a handful of cocoa beans and toast them on a griddle. Crack open the shells and remove the cocoa nibs. Grind the nibs in a mortar and pestle to a smooth paste and then stir in some freshly ground black pepper and ground corn. Take about a teaspoon of the paste and add enough water to make a large glass. Sweeten with sugar to taste. The Maya vary this drink by adding spices such as cinnamon, allspice, and nutmeg.

HINT: Be warned. *Kukuh* is a very different drink to our traditional
sweet and creamy hot chocolate drink.

This cake is light and moist, and the flavor of the chocolate and the almonds together with the texture and taste of the figs combine to make it truly unforgettable. Rachael Vingoe sent us this recipe, inspired by a cake that she bakes each Christmas.

CHOCOLATE, FIG, AND ALMOND
CAKE

Preparation time: 20 minutes
Baking time: 50 minutes
Use: 9-inch springform cake pan

5 ounces dried ready-to-eat figs (about 1 cup)

3 tablespoons Amaretto

1 cup plus 2 tablespoons (2$^{1}/_{4}$ sticks) unsalted butter, softened

1$^{1}/_{4}$ cups sugar

3 ounces ground almonds (about $^{1}/_{3}$ cup)

$^{3}/_{4}$ cup flour

4 large eggs

two 3$^{1}/_{2}$-oz. bars dark chocolate, minimum 60% cocoa content, chopped

3 heaped tablespoons cocoa powder

4 ounces whole peeled almonds (about $^{3}/_{4}$ cup)

Preheat the oven to 350°F. Butter and line the cake pan with parchment paper. Alternatively, butter the pan and dust with ground almonds to coat, shaking out any excess.

Remove the hard stalks from the figs and chop the figs in a food processor into very small pieces. Place in a small bowl and pour the Amaretto over them. Set aside.

Cream the butter and the sugar until light and fluffy. Mix the ground almonds with the flour in a separate bowl. In another bowl, beat the eggs and add a little at a time to the butter mixture, beating gently between each addition. (If you are using an electric beater, it should be on its slowest speed.) Then add the almonds and flour, a third at a time, continuing to beat gently.

Carefully fold in the chopped chocolate, the figs, and Amaretto to the batter.

Spoon the batter into the cake pan and smooth over the top using a butter knife. Dust the top evenly with two heaped tablespoons of the cocoa. Arrange the peeled almonds on top and then bake the cake for 40 to 50 minutes or until it is firm to the touch and a skewer inserted in the center comes out clean. Let cool and then use a wire mesh strainer to sprinkle the remaining cocoa over the top before serving.

HINT: Serve with freshly chopped coconut stirred into whipped cream.

If you are ever in Paris, treat yourself to tea in the beautiful dining rooms at Ladurée on the Champs Élysées. Don't be put off by the lines of people waiting and don't leave without an exquisitely wrapped box of the most famous macaroons in Paris.

CHOCOLATE
MACAROONS

Preparation time: 20 minutes
Cooking time: 10–12 minutes
Use: 2 large cookie sheets, large pastry bag with ³/₄-inch nozzle

4¹/₂ ounces ground almonds (about 1¹/₃ cups)

¹/₄ cup cocoa powder

2¹/₄ cups confectioners' sugar

3 large egg whites, at room temperature

¹/₄ teaspoon vanilla extract

2 tablespoons cocoa powder for dusting

GANACHE

see Micah's Truffles, page 147

Preheat the oven to 475°F.

Butter the cookie sheets and then line them with parchment paper with an overlap of about an inch at either end. Prepare your pastry bag and nozzle.

Sift together the ground almonds, cocoa, and two cups of the confectioners' sugar (reserving a quarter-cup of the confectioners' sugar for the egg whites).

Measure out exactly a scant half-cup of the egg whites, setting aside any excess whites for another use.

In a large bowl, beat the egg whites until they are light and fluffy, add the reserved confectioners' sugar and continue to whisk until they are stiff and shiny but not dry. Gently fold the dry ingredients into the egg whites. Let rest for 10 minutes.

Stir the vanilla extract into the mixture, allowing it to deflate a little. This will help to stop the macaroons from cracking on top. Pour the mixture into the pastry bag. Pipe the mixture onto the cookie sheets in cookies the size of walnuts – try to make them as regular as possible. Tap the bottoms of the cookie sheets on a flat surface to remove some more of the air from the macaroons. Sprinkle some cocoa on top of each one.

Put the first cookie sheet on the top shelf of the oven and bake for one minute, and then reduce the temperature to 350°F. Cook the macaroons for another 10 to 12 minutes or until they are obviously cooked but not gooey and are still soft to the touch.

About one minute after you have removed the cookie sheet from the oven, gently lift one end of the paper and immediately pour a splash of hot water under the paper. The hot baking sheet causes the water to form steam and makes it easy to remove the macaroons. Carefully peel the macaroons from the paper and place on a wire rack to cool. Repeat the process with the second batch.

Once the macaroons have cooled, sandwich two together with the Ganache.

HINT: The secret is to use "old" egg whites that have been kept uncovered in a fridge for at least a week.

Dodi Miller is passionate about chiles and is the driving force behind the company that has made the greatest variety and best-quality chiles available in the UK. She is also passionate about her Mole Poblano recipe and explains that it is a dish that can take a couple of days to prepare and that it is made for people you love, usually for festive occasions. There are many moles: green, red, yellow, and black, but Poblano, the one with chocolate, is the most famous. The chocolate is used as a spice; it rounds off the edges of the chiles and gives the sauce a deep richness.

COOL CHILE Co.

MOLE POBLANO DE GUAJOLOTE

(dark chile, nut, and chocolate mole with turkey)

Preparation time: 2 hours
Cooking time: 1¹/₂ hours. Best left for a day before eating
Use: stockpot, large ovenproof pan
Serves: 8-10. For 12–16 use a 9–11 pound turkey and double the quantities for the mole

5–6¹/₂ pound turkey (or a large chicken; the long slow cooking suits robust free-range birds)

STOCK INGREDIENTS

1 onion

1 carrot

1 stalk celery

1 bay leaf

dried thyme

salt

pepper

MOLE

1 large beef tomato, roasted under the broiler so the skin blackens, core removed

2 tablespoons sesame seeds, dry toasted

2 tablespoons coriander seeds, dry toasted

1¹/₂ ounces dark chocolate, minimum 60% cocoa content, grated (about ¹/₂ cup)

4¹/₂ ounces dried mulato chiles

1¹/₂ ounces dried ancho chiles

1¹/₄ ounces dried pasilla chiles

¹/₃ cup duck/goose fat or lard, melted, or vegetable oil

¹/₃ cup whole almonds, skin on

3 tablespoons raisins

1 small onion, peeled and chopped

2 garlic cloves, peeled and chopped

2 whole cloves (or pinch of ground clove)

5 peppercorns (or ¹/₄ teaspoon ground black pepper)

¹/₂ teaspoon ground cinnamon

2 stale corn tortillas or 2 stale pieces bread (or use 2 tablespoons masa harina)

1 teaspoon salt

2 tablespoons sugar

¹/₄ teaspoon ground anise (or 1 star anise)

sesame seeds, for garnishing

Ask your butcher to cut up the turkey, saving the carcass, trimmings, and giblets to make the stock. You can also do this yourself: remove the wings, legs, thighs, and breasts with the bones in, wrap, and keep in the refrigerator. Put the carcass, wing tips, and giblets into a stockpot, cover with water, add the stock ingredients, simmer for two hours, partially covered, then skim and strain to produce a rich, tasty stock.

To make the mole, chop the roasted tomato and put it into a bowl, along with the toasted sesame and coriander seeds and the grated chocolate.

To prepare the dried chiles, wipe off any dirt with a barely damp cloth. Pull out the stem and run your finger down the side to open the chile out flat, shake out all the seeds, and remove the membranes attaching them. Make a pile of the flat chile pieces. Heat two tablespoons of the melted fat or oil in a frying pan over medium-high heat. Fry the chile pieces one at a time for just a few seconds on either side; the color will become tan. Do not overdo this, as the chiles will become very bitter. Drain as much of the fat back into the pan as you lift out the chiles and put them into a separate bowl. When you have finished frying all the chiles cover them with just boiled water using a weighted bowl to keep them submerged. Put to one side and soak for one hour, then drain.

Using the pan that you fried the chiles in, add a little more fat, if necessary, and fry the almonds until golden, drain and add to the bowl containing the chopped tomato. Next fry the raisins until they puff, drain them and add to the bowl, then fry the onions and garlic until brown, drain and add to the bowl. Add the cloves, black pepper, and cinnamon to the pan, fry for one minute and then add them to the bowl as well. Lastly tear the stale corn tortillas into pieces, fry,

drain, and add them to the bowl, or else, scoop out a little of the tomato mixture and mix the masa harina into it and then stir it back into the bowl.

Put a quarter of the tomato mixture and about a third-cup of stock into a blender and blend until smooth. Strain into a clean bowl and continue blending the tomato mixture and stock, adding only enough stock to produce a thick paste, until the tomato mixture is used up.

Next purée the drained chiles, a quarter of them at a time, adding a third-cup stock so they blend easily. Strain into a separate bowl. Do this until all the chiles have been puréed.

Pat the turkey pieces dry using paper towel. Heat two tablespoons of the melted fat or oil in a pot and brown the turkey on all sides, working in batches if necessary. Remove the pieces to a large casserole dish.

When complete, drain away most of the fat, leaving a little, and reheat the pan. Add the chile purée, stirring all the time, letting it bubble, darken and thicken. This takes about five minutes. Then add the tomato-based purée and simmer for about two minutes. Add three cups of the stock, reduce the heat and simmer the sauce for 45 minutes. Then add a teaspoon salt and two tablespoons sugar, or to taste. The sauce should coat the back of a spoon – add a little more stock if it is too thick.

Preheat the oven to 350°F. Pour the sauce over the turkey pieces, add the anise or star anise, cover with a lid or foil and place in the oven for one and a half hours until the turkey is tender.

Serve sprinkled with toasted sesame seeds, accompanied with rice, corn tortillas, and a watercress salad. Be generous with the sauce over the turkey.

HINT: When cooking with dried chiles, it is best to weigh them rather than counting them or measuring them in cups, as they vary so much in size.

WICKED

The rain forest is the perfect environment for the cacao tree, which likes rich soil, humidity, and shade.
It is rare to find *Theobroma cacao* growing outside a band 20 degrees north and 20 degrees south of the Equator.

Angela Reid remembers making this recipe with her grandmother in late September when she used to decant the damson gin to make way for the coming year's batch. The fruit left behind was so good you just could not throw it away. This is Angela's favorite of the many recipes devised to use up the drunken damsons. If you are not using damsons rescued from your own damson gin, we have adapted this recipe so that you can use fresh plums instead as we have done.

DRUNKEN DAMSON

DESSERT

Preparation time: 20 minutes if you have damson gin, 2 hours, 20 minutes if making with plums
Cooking time: 12 minutes for a pie, 6 minutes for ramekins or custard cups
Use: 8-inch shallow pie dish or 8 ramekins
Serves: 8

DRUNKEN PLUMS
(if you are not using your own damsons in gin)

8 large plums, pitted and cut in half

2 tablespoons water

$1/4$ cup sugar

$1/4$ cup gin

FILLING

$1/2$ cup sugar

8 medium eggs

18 ounces dark chocolate,
minimum 60% cocoa content, broken into pieces

1 cup plus 2 tablespoons unsalted butter ($2^1/4$ cups)

if you are not using the plums above:
7 ounces pitted damsons in gin (about 1–$1^1/2$ cups)

Preheat the oven to 400°F. Butter the pie dish or ramekins.

To make the drunken plums, poach them gently in the sugar and water for about 10 minutes. Remove from the heat, stir in the gin, and let cool and marinate for about two hours.

Beat together the eggs and sugar until pale and creamy. Melt the chocolate and butter in the top of a double boiler suspended over barely simmering water. Mix the chocolate mixture and the drained fruit into the egg and sugar batter. Pour into the dish or divide between the ramekins ensuring that there is fruit in each one.

Bake for 12 minutes for the pie dish or six minutes for the ramekins, until firm to the touch, but still slightly wobbly. Let cool and serve with your favorite cream.

HINT: If you are tempted to drizzle a little left-over gin over this dessert, beware.
It is far too strong and will overwhelm the chocolate and fruit flavors.

WICKED

White Chocolate

When we make our Dark Chocolate with 70% cocoa content, we begin by mixing together cocoa liquor, raw cane sugar, and Bourbon vanilla to our own special recipe.

This mixture is then refined through a series of rollers that grind the particles of cocoa, sugar, and vanilla so finely that they cannot be felt on the tongue. This process also continues to develop the flavor of the chocolate.

The next stage is the conching, which cannot be hurried and is a vital stage in the production of quality chocolate. A conching vessel, named after the conch shell-shape of the first prototype, controls the temperature and stirs the chocolate to create a smooth, velvety texture. The volatile acids are driven off and the flavor of the chocolate matures.

Extra cocoa butter is added at the end of conching to make the chocolate super smooth and to help it to melt more easily in the mouth.

Some chocolates are made using cheaper fats that are derived from nut and palm oil, which leaves a greasy film in the mouth.

The ultimate indulgence after a cold walk, this recipe can be made simpler by omitting the cinnamon or the cream but the drink will be less rich.

LUXURY

COCOA

Preparation time: 15 minutes
Makes: 1 standard mug

1 cup whole milk

2 tablespoons heavy cream

2 sticks cinnamon, about 2 inches long

1 tablespoon cocoa powder

about 2 teaspoons unrefined cane sugar
(or sugar of your choice)

Put the milk, cream, and cinnamon sticks in a pan and slowly bring to a boil. Once it's reached a boil, turn off the heat and let the cinnamon infuse — for a faint cinnamon flavor, leave the sticks in for just a few minutes; for a fuller cinnamon flavor, leave them in for 10 minutes.

When you are ready to serve the cocoa, reheat the milk mixture and while it heats, spoon the cocoa powder into your mug, add enough of the milk mixture to form a paste, and stir.

When the milk mixture has just reached a boil, pour it into your mug, stirring to blend the cocoa paste with the milk. Add sugar to taste, and stir well.

Retrieve the infused cinnamon sticks and submerge in the cocoa, if you like.

HINT: If you like cardamom, try substituting the cinnamon with the black seeds
from inside one or two green cardamom pods, slightly crushed with the back of a spoon.
Let the seeds infuse for 10 minutes before reheating, then strain the mixture into the mug.

White chocolate is one of those things that people either love or loathe, but good-quality white chocolate made with real vanilla and cocoa butter will taste very different to the flavor most people are accustomed to. Not surprisingly, children love this sweet recipe from Jenny Phillips.

BANANA
AND WHITE CHOCOLATE CAKE

Preparation time: 20 minutes
Cooking time: 35 minutes
Use: two 7-inch cake pans

CAKE

³/₄ cup (1¹/₂ sticks) unsalted butter

³/₄ cup sugar

3 large eggs

2 ripe bananas, mashed

2 cups self-rising flour
(if you do not have self-rising flour, then use all-purpose flour, increase the baking powder to 3¹/₂ teaspoons, and add 1 tablespoon salt.)

¹/₂ teaspoon baking powder

FILLING

2 bananas

juice of 1 lemon

1 tablespoon rosewater

²/₃ cup crème fraîche or sour cream

ICING

two 3¹/₂-oz. bars good-quality white chocolate, broken into pieces

3 tablespoons unsalted butter

Preheat the oven to 350°F. Brush the baking pans with melted butter and dust with flour.

Cream together the butter and sugar, and beat in the eggs and the mashed banana. Sift the flour and baking powder into the mixture and fold in well.

Divide the batter between the two pans and bake for about 40 minutes. Leave the cakes in the pans for 10 minutes, then turn out onto a wire rack to cool.

To make the filling, slice the bananas very thinly and toss in the lemon juice.

Mix the rosewater into the crème fraîche and spread this onto one of the cooled cake layers, top with the sliced bananas, and sandwich the two cakes together.

Melt the white chocolate and the butter in the top of a double boiler suspended over barely simmering water.

Spread the melted chocolate mixture evenly over the top and sides of the cake, starting by pouring it into the center of the top of the cake and spreading it with a butter knife until it begins to dribble down the sides of the cake.

Hint: Use fresh flowers placed in a test tube to decorate your cake.
Chocolate Cosmos has a wonderful chocolate scent and deep brown colour,
while shockingly pink sweet peas look beautiful with a chocolate glaze.

What would we do without those little books crammed with recipes from enthusiastic cooks compiled to raise money for schools and charities? This recipe, from the Bergvliet Road Nursery School in Cape Town, South Africa, has that Sixties ring to it – it is sweet and very rich and, along with a cup of tea, is guaranteed to hit the spot.

COFFEE, CHOCOLATE
AND WALNUT CAKE

Preparation time: 25 minutes
Cooking time: 25 minutes
Use: two 7-inch round cake pans
Serves 10

2 cups (4 sticks) unsalted butter

1 cup light brown sugar

4 large eggs

1 cup minus 2 tablespoons strong fresh coffee, cooled

4 teaspoons cocoa powder

1²/₃ cups self-rising flour

1¹/₂ cups walnuts, chopped

walnuts for decorating

FROSTING

Nigella's Blond Icing (see page 181)

Preheat the oven to 375°F. Butter and flour the two pans.

Cream the butter and sugar until light and fluffy, add the eggs, one at a time, beating well between each addition. Mix in the coffee. Sift the cocoa and self-rising flour together and add to the mixture, beating everything well. Don't worry if the mixture has curdled slightly as it will come together once baked. Fold in the chopped walnuts and divide the mixture between the two pans. Bake in the oven for 25 minutes. Let cool in the pans for a few minutes before turning out and transferring to a wire rack to cool completely. When the cakes have cooled, place one cake layer on a plate and frost the top and sides. Place the other cake on top and frost its top and sides. Decorate with walnut pieces.

Hint: This cake should be handled carefully as it can break easily.

WICKED

"Folks who like to fume and fuss are like a rocking chair; they use a lot of energy but don't get anywhere." Kim Potter's great-aunt Lucille wrote *A Collection of 62 Years of Marriage*, a book of recipes and some wonderful words of wisdom. She was a sweet and strong-willed lady who, well into her nineties, thought nothing of jumping into her car and driving hundreds of miles. This is one of Kim's favorite recipes, adapted to include chocolate.

AUNT LUCILLE'S
PUMPKIN & MAYA GOLD BREAD

Preparation time: 30 minutes
Cooking time: 50 minutes–1 hour
Use: 9 x 5-inch loaf pan
Makes: 1 loaf (14 slices)

1¹/₂ cups granulated sugar

¹/₄ cup (¹/₂ stick) unsalted butter, softened

2 large eggs

8 ounces peeled and grated raw pumpkin or butternut squash (about 2 cups)

3 cups all-purpose flour

¹/₂ teaspoon baking soda

¹/₂ teaspoon salt

¹/₂ teaspoon baking powder

¹/₂ teaspoon ground nutmeg

¹/₂ teaspoon allspice

¹/₂ teaspoon cinnamon

¹/₄ teaspoon ground cloves

¹/₄ cup water

2 ounces Maya Gold, or other good-quality, dark, orange-flavored chocolate, chopped

Preheat the oven to 350°F. Brush the loaf pan with melted butter and dust with flour.

Cream the butter and sugar until light and fluffy. Add the eggs, one at a time, beating well between each addition, then add the grated pumpkin and mix well.

Sift together the flour, baking soda, salt, baking powder, and all the spices, and stir into the pumpkin mixture alternating with the water, until everything is incorporated.

Spoon about half the batter into the loaf pan. Sprinkle about half the chocolate pieces on top of the batter then cover them with the remaining batter. Dig into the batter with a spoon, parting it to form a trench along the top of the loaf, and fill with the remaining chocolate, letting some of the chocolate remain on top of the loaf. Smooth over the hole with the spoon. The chocolate will melt as the loaf cooks and create a fault line through the loaf.

Bake in the oven for 50 minutes to one hour. Cover with foil after 30 minutes to prevent the top from burning. Depending upon how moist your pumpkin is, you may need to bake this bread for a little longer. Test by inserting a skewer into the center: if it comes out clean (although there might be melted chocolate left on the skewer), the loaves are cooked. Turn onto a wire rack and let cool before serving.

HINT: This loaf is delicious when sliced and lightly toasted with butter.
The easiest way to grate the pumpkin or squash is to use the grater attachment on your food processor.

"You may lose the thread of your thoughts when you savor one of these sun-filled Mediterranean dates," writes Marialuisa Rea Faggionato from Padua in Italy. She stuffs the dates with an orange-and lemon-flavored marzipan, coats them in dark chocolate, and serves them chilled for dessert. Marialuisa was a runner-up in one of our recipe competitions.

MEDITERRANEAN

THOUGHT-STEALING DATES

Preparation time: 30 minutes
Cooling time: 30 minutes
Use: wire rack
Makes: 30

30 dates

$^1/_2$ cup peeled whole almonds

$^1/_4$ cup superfine sugar

finely grated zest of 1 orange,
plus a little of the juice

4 teaspoons Limoncello
(Italian liqueur flavored with lemon zest)

5 ounces dark chocolate,
minimum 60% cocoa content, broken into pieces

Remove the pits from the dates. Chop the almonds finely and mix them with the sugar and orange zest. Add the Limoncello and knead to a malleable marzipan, adding a little orange juice if needed. Stuff the dates with the marzipan mixture.

Melt the chocolate in the top of a double boiler over barely simmering water. Dip the ends of the dates into the chocolate, leaving the center bare, or dunk them to coat completely. Dip them twice if you like. Leave them in a cool place to harden before serving.

HINT: Try to use fresh dates for this recipe, but if you can't find them, choose dates that have been coated in as little syrup as possible.

This recipe started life as an almond tart with strawberries. They were replaced by pears, then chocolate was added, and lastly the ginger appeared. Hazel Neil likes to adapt recipes depending upon seasonal availability and the contents of her pantry. Next time she will try plums.

CHOCOLATE, PEAR, AND GINGER
TART

Preparation time: 40 minutes
Chilling time: 30 minutes
Cooking time: 1 hour
Use: 11-inch removable-bottomed fluted tart pan
Serves: 8

PIE DOUGH

2 cups all-purpose flour

1 teaspoon salt

$1/2$ cup (1 stick) unsalted butter

2 large egg yolks

4–5 tablespoons cold water

FILLING

$1/2$ cup (1 stick) unsalted butter

$1/2$ cup sugar

2 large eggs

one 3$1/2$-oz. bar dark chocolate, minimum 60% cocoa content, broken into pieces

1 tablespoon finely chopped preserved ginger in syrup

3 tablespoons all-purpose flour

1$1/3$ cups ground almonds

4 pears, just ripe, peeled

apricot jam for glaze

FOR SERVING

Simple Chocolate Sauce, see page 61

Preheat the oven to 350°F.

To make the pie dough, sift the flour and salt into a large bowl. Cut the butter up into chunks and rub into the flour using your fingers until it resembles bread crumbs. In a small bowl, whisk together the egg yolks and the cold water briefly and then add to the mixture. Mix together until they come together as a ball. Wrap the dough in waxed paper and leave in the fridge to rest for about 30 minutes, before rolling out to line your tart pan. Bake the pastry blind by covering it with foil and filling with dried beans for about 15 to 20 minutes or until lightly colored.

Remove the pie crust from the oven and lower the temperature to 325°F.

To make the filling, cream the butter and sugar until light and fluffy. Beat the eggs, then add them slowly and mix well. Melt the chocolate in the top of a double boiler over barely simmering water. Let cool for a few minutes. Add the chocolate to the mixture along with the ginger. Mix in the flour and the almonds. Let cool before spreading over the pastry botto of the pie crust.

Cut the pears in half, remove the cores, and slice into wedges. Arrange in a fan shape on top of the chocolate mixture and press in slightly. Bake for about 30 to 40 minutes. Test that the filling is cooked by inserting a skewer into the center which should come out clean.

Brush with apricot jam while still warm and serve warm or cold, with chocolate sauce or cream.

Andrea Longman invented these crumbly and buttery slices for a vegan friend as a thank-you present. They can be made with vegan margarine and are now a regular feature of her Christmas cookie cooking bonanza and are her friend's favorite Christmas present. If you make these for children, use milk chocolate instead.

SCRUMMY

CHOCOLATE SWIRL SHORTBREAD

Preparation time: 20 minutes
Cooking time: 25 minutes
Use: cookie sheet
Makes: 14

SHORTBREAD 1

1 cup all-purpose flour

$1/2$ teaspoon salt

$1/4$ cup sugar

$1/2$ cup (1 stick) unsalted butter or vegan margarine

SHORTBREAD 2

1 cup all-purpose flour

$1/4$ cup cocoa powder

$1/2$ teaspoon salt

$1/4$ cup sugar

$1/2$ cup (1 stick) unsalted butter or vegan margarine

one $3^1/2$-oz. bar dark chocolate,
minimum 60% cocoa content, or milk chocolate,
preferably 34% cocoa content, chopped into pieces

Preheat the oven to 300°F.

To make the first shortbread, sift together the flour, salt, and sugar. Rub in the butter until the mixture combines. Knead lightly, then place the dough in the fridge for 30 minutes before rolling out.

Follow the same step for the second shortbread, but include the cocoa with the flour.

Roll out each dough on a lightly floured surface into equal-sized rectangles about a half-inch thick. Place the plain shortbread on a sheet of waxed paper, place the chocolate shortbread on top of the plain one and then put the bigger pieces of chocolate onto the middle of the shortbread and scatter the smaller shards over the rest of the surface.

Carefully roll the shortbread like a Swiss roll, as tightly as possible, using the waxed paper to support it. (Don't worry if it breaks or the chocolate pokes through.) Once rolled, pinch both ends together to prevent the chocolate falling out, then using both hands, squeeze until it is about eight inches long.

Using a very sharp knife, slice the roll into half-inch slices. Line a cookie sheet with parchment paper, or grease the cookie sheet with butter. Lay the cookies on the cookie sheet, leaving plenty of room in between. Bake for 25 minutes, or until the plain shortbread has darkened slightly to a light golden color. Cool on a wire rack.

HINT: These biscuits are clumsy and rustic-looking rather than elegant.

A British specialty dating back to the Middle Ages, fruit cakes have been baked for celebrations, weddings, and at Christmas since the early eighteenth century. This twist on a traditional fruit cake is a bewitching creation by Stuart Oetzmann. His bakery, The Handmade Food Company, supplies the classiest food outlets in England with the most exquisite pies and pastries.

FRUIT
CAKE

Preparation time: 1 hour
Cooking time: 1 hour, 15 minutes
Macerating time: 24 hours in advance
Use: two 9 x 5-inch loaf pans

³/₄ cup raisins

¹/₂ cup currants

1¹/₂ cups pitted prunes

³/₄ cup candied orange, lemon, or grapefruit peel (preferably homemade)

¹/₂ cup brandy

¹/₄ cup Morgan's Spiced Rum

1¹/₄ cups (2¹/₂ sticks) unsalted butter, softened

1³/₄ cups muscovado sugar or dark brown sugar

3 medium eggs

1¹/₂ cups self-rising flour

1 cup all-purpose flour

1 teaspoon cinnamon

¹/₄ teaspoon mace

¹/₄ teaspoon ground cloves

¹/₄ teaspoon ground ginger

¹/₂ cup espresso coffee

1 cup walnuts

9 ounces dark chocolate, minimum 60% cocoa content, broken into pieces

Soak the fruit in half the brandy and all of the rum, 24 hours before cooking.

Preheat the oven to 325°F.

Butter the pans and line with foil or parchment paper.

Cream the butter and sugar. Add the eggs, one at a time, beating thoroughly each time, making sure the egg is well incorporated before adding the next. Sift the flours and spices together. Add to the batter in two stages, combining well between each addition. Fold in the fruit and the coffee. Finally add the walnuts and chocolate and mix thoroughly. Divide between the two pans, cover loosely with parchment paper and make a hole the size of a quarter in the top of the paper to let the steam escape. Cover with foil, making another hole, and tucking it under at the sides. Bake for one hour and a quarter hours, checking the cake after about an hour. A skewer inserted into the center should come out dry, with a few crumbs clinging to the tip.

Let the cakes cool in their pans for 30 minutes and then turn out, peel off the paper, and pour the remaining brandy on top.

HINT: If you are making this several months in advance for a special occasion, douse it regularly with brandy, and keep it wrapped in foil.

This pudding is a mint chocolate-lover's dream dessert with its light soufflé texture and warm sauce oozing from the center. Nicola Oaten started baking chocolate cakes at the age of five and has been experimenting ever since. This is her favorite recipe.

MINI HOT CHOCOLATE PUDDINGS

WITH A HINT OF MINT

Preparation time: 30 minutes
Cooking time: 10 minutes
Use: 4 small pudding bowls or dariole molds, 2$\frac{1}{2}$-inch diameter and 2 inches deep
Serves: 4

2 ounces dark chocolate, minimum 60% cocoa content, broken into pieces

$\frac{1}{3}$ cup ($\frac{3}{4}$ stick) unsalted butter

2 large eggs

2 large egg yolks

2 tablespoons light brown sugar

2 ounces mint fondant chocolate

6 tablespoons all-purpose flour

cocoa powder and confectioners' sugar, for dusting

Preheat the oven to 425°F if you intend to cook the puddings as soon as they are prepared. If you are cooking the puddings from frozen, preheat the oven to 350°F. Lightly butter and flour the pudding bowls or dariole moulds.

Put the chocolate and butter in the top of a double boiler over barely simmering water. Heat until the chocolate begins to melt, then turn off the heat. Continue to stir until melted and then let cool.

Meanwhile put the eggs and egg yolks in a bowl along with the sugar and beat until frothy. When the chocolate mixture has cooled, fold it into the egg mixture. Sift in the flour and fold again. Pour into the prepared molds filling them to the top, level off with a butter knife and bake for 10 minutes, if serving immediately. Alternatively, they can be frozen, or stored in the fridge for up to one day. Puddings cooked directly from the fridge will need an extra two minutes in the oven at 425°F, frozen puddings need 12 minutes at 350°F. The puddings will rise and be soft and gooey in the middle when ready.

Loosen from the molds using a knife and turn out into the palm of your hand, then place them right-side up on individual plates. Dust with a mixture of cocoa powder and confectioners' sugar.

HINT: Fill the molds right to the top for a tall, elegant pudding.

WICKED

At Green & Black's we prefer the French style of truffle which is predominantly a chocolate ganache, dusted with cocoa powder. They were first called truffles in the 1920s because they looked like real, freshly dug truffles, which are a fungus whose fruiting body grows underground. Belgian truffles often have a sweet, soft, light and creamy center, which is very rich and filling.

MICAH'S
TRUFFLES

Preparation time: 30 minutes
Chilling time: minimum 3 hours or overnight
Makes: 36

10 ounces dark chocolate, minimum 60% cocoa content, broken into pieces

1 cup heavy cream

$^1/_4$ cup ($^1/_2$ stick) unsalted butter, at room temperature

$^1/_2$ cup cocoa powder

Place the chocolate in a large bowl. In a saucepan, bring the cream to a boil and pour it over the chocolate. Stir gently until the chocolate has melted, trying not to create bubbles. Let cool for two minutes, then add the butter in two stages and stir in gently. Once the butter is incorporated, the ganache should be smooth and glossy with no oil slick on the surface. Set the truffle mixture in the fridge for a minimum of three hours or overnight.

Remove the ganache from the fridge about 15 minutes before you want to make the truffles, depending upon room temperature. Put the cocoa into a bowl. Ensure your hands are cold and dry, then dust your hands with cocoa. Take spoonfuls of the ganache mixture (use a teaspoon or a tablespoon, depending upon how large you like your truffles) and roll the mixture into a ball in your cocoa-dusted hands. Drop each shaped truffle into the bowl of cocoa, turn it around to coat, and then toss it between your palms to remove any excess powder. The truffles can then be returned to the fridge and kept for up to two days, as long as they are stored in an airtight container.

HINT: These truffles can be eaten directly from the fridge or allowed to come to room temperature. The colder the truffle, the less dry and dusty the cocoa will seem when eating it.

ABRACADABRA

The complex flavor of chocolate is created by 550 flavor compounds found in cocoa after fermentation, drying, roasting, and conching – far more than in most foods. A carrot has 96 flavor compounds.

GOLD

CHOCOLATE
GREEN & BLACK'S

Fairtrade

Guarantees
a better deal
For Third World
Producers

SOIL ASSOCIATION
ORGANIC STANDARD

LAO

TEMPERING

To mold chocolate or cover a cake in a hard chocolate shell that will set with a glossy shine, you have to temper the chocolate first, in exactly the same way we mold our chocolate bars.

Tempering involves melting, cooling, and then reheating the chocolate, ensuring that all the tiny fat crystals in the chocolate are stable. If the fat crystals are not stable, the chocolate will set with white streaks or bloom. It will also be dull and won't have a good snap – the sound that good chocolate makes when you break it.

HOW TO TEMPER CHOCOLATE

To temper chocolate you need to use a minimum of $10\frac{1}{2}$ ounces of dark, milk, or white chocolate (three $3\frac{1}{2}$-oz. bars). Any excess can always be stored and re-used another time.

Grate about a half-cup of chocolate and set it aside. Break the remainder of the chocolate into pieces and melt in the top of a double boiler over gently simmering water; if using the alternative method described on page 9, do not let the bottom of the bowl come into direct contact with the water. Once the chocolate is completely melted, check the temperature using a digital thermometer. It should be between 131 to 136°F for dark chocolate, 113 to 122°F for milk and white chocolate.

Remove the chocolate from the heat and place over a bowl of cold water at about 70°F. Let cool, while occasionally stirring, until the temperature of the chocolate drops to 93°F.

Gently stir in the reserved grated chocolate and continue stirring until all the chocolate has melted and the temperature has cooled to 89 to 91°F.

The final temperature for dark chocolate should be about 86 to 90°F, between 82 to 86°F for milk, and 82 to 84°F for white chocolate.

To test whether you have tempered your chocolate correctly, dip the tip of a butter knife in the chocolate and then let it cool and set for about five minutes. Properly tempered chocolate will be smooth with an even color on the top, and if you peel the chocolate off the knife, the bottom will appear shiny. You can always start again using the same chocolate if you have failed to temper it properly.

Use the tempered chocolate immediately and quickly, leaving it over a pan of warm water while you work with it.

For a less technical method, see page 9.

ABRACADABRA

This impressive, rich, chocolate cake is incredibly easy to make and guaranteed to launch your guests into orbit. It can also be made by replacing some of the dark chocolate with Maya Gold Chocolate, to give the cake a hint of orange and spice. For an extra-special occasion, shake or brush edible gold dust (available from specialty cooking stores) over it.

DARK CHOCOLATE MOUSSE CAKE
WITH GOLD DUST

Preparation time: 10 minutes
Cooking time: 35–45 minutes
Use: 8- or 9-inch springform cake pan with removable base or a similar-sized removable-bottomed tart pan
Serves: 10

1 tablespoon ground almonds, plus extra for dusting the pan

three 3¹/₂-oz. bars dark chocolate, minimum 60% cocoa content
or two 3¹/₂-oz. bars dark chocolate and one 3¹/₂-oz. bar Maya Gold Chocolate, or other good-quality dark, orange-flavored chocolate, broken into pieces

1¹/₂ cups sugar

²/₃ cup (1¹/₄ sticks) unsalted butter

pinch of sea salt

5 large eggs

confectioners' sugar or gold dust

Preheat the oven to 350°F. Brush the pan with a little melted butter and dust with the ground almonds, shaking off any excess.

Melt the chocolate, sugar, butter, and salt in the top of a double boiler over barely simmering water, then remove from the heat.

Beat the eggs with the ground almonds and fold into the chocolate mixture. The batter will thicken after a few minutes. Pour into the cake pan and bake for 35 to 40 minutes.

Remove the sides of the pan and leave the cake on the bottom part to cool, then dust using a sifter with confectioners' sugar or brush with edible gold dust.

HINT: This cake will not rise much – it should be rich and thin.
If chilled overnight it will be dense, fudgey, and wicked!

Micah Carr-Hill, our chocolate taster and product development chef, came back from one of his many forays in Italy with this dreamy idea. He visited the "Salone del Gusto," a food fair that takes place in Turin every other autumn, and spent one evening at a dinner that had a chocolate theme. Make sure your Gorgonzola dolce is perfectly ripe, not too runny and not too hard, and don't be afraid to pile on the chopped chocolate. The idea is that you taste the Gorgonzola first and then the chocolate begins to melt in your mouth and cuts through the richness, leaving you in a state of calm ecstasy.

GORGONZOLA DOLCE
WITH DARK CHOCOLATE

Preparation time: 5 minutes
Makes: 60 pieces

one 3½-oz. bar dark chocolate, minimum 60% cocoa content

12 ounces Gorgonzola dolce

Chop the chocolate into medium-sized chunks, about the size of your thumbnail, using a sharp knife.

Cover the entire surface of the cheese with the chunks of chocolate, pressing it in gently.

Make sure that the cheese is densely covered, as you do need a high proportion of chocolate to cheese to get the full benefit of this recipe.

HINT: Don't store your cheese in the fridge because if the temperature is too low, the cold can impair the flavor. Wrap it in waxed paper or parchment paper and store it in a cool place.

Sally Johnston's brother-in-law had never tried to cook before he spent some time in a Canadian prison. A fellow prisoner gave him this simple recipe to cook for his wife when she visited him and it has since become a family favorite. He sent it to Sally in England and she passed it on to us.

INMATES'
CHOCOLATE CAKE

Preparation time: 20 minutes
Cooking time: 40 minutes
Use: two 8-inch cake pans with deep sides
Serves: 15–20

CAKE

3³/₄ cups all-purpose flour

2¹/₃ cups sugar

1 teaspoon baking soda

1 tablespoon baking powder

¹/₂ teaspoon salt

1¹/₂ cups cocoa powder

²/₃ cup buttermilk

²/₃ cup vegetable oil

4 large eggs

1 teaspoon vanilla extract

1 cup minus 2 tablespoons water

FILLING

12 ounces apricot jam (about 1¹/₂ cups)

chocolate glaze (see page 180) or
chocolate fudge sauce (see page 61)

Preheat the oven to 350°F. Butter and flour the baking pans.

Sift all the dry ingredients into a large mixing bowl. Add the remaining ingredients and beat using an electric beater or with a strong arm for about three minutes. Bake for 35 to 40 minutes. Let cool on a wire rack. Once cooled, sandwich together with apricot jam and pour the chocolate glaze over the cake.

HINT: If you are in a hurry, use two large jars of chocolate spread to frost this cake.

A great classic, this recipe was picked up in the Eighties in Paris and originated in the famous Taillevent restaurant. It is delicious served with Mint Crème Anglaise (see page 61) and tuiles.

TAILLEVENT
TERRINE

Preparation time: 20 minutes
Freezing time: overnight
Use: 1-pound loaf pan

8 ounces dark chocolate,
minimum 60% cocoa content, broken into pieces

1 cup confectioners' sugar

³/₄ cup (1¹/₂ sticks) softened unsalted butter

5 large eggs, separated

1 cup cocoa powder

salt

³/₄ cup whipping cream

Melt the chocolate in the top of a double boiler over barely simmering water.

Scoop the melted chocolate into a large bowl, add the confectioners' sugar, and stir to combine. Cream in the softened butter. add the egg yolks, cocoa, and a pinch of salt, and beat until mixed. In a separate bowl, beat the egg whites until soft peaks form. In another bowl, whip the cream until thick. Alternate folding the beaten whites and the whipped cream into the chocolate batter, ensuring they are well incorporated after each addition.

Sprinkle water inside the loaf pan, line with plastic wrap, pour the mixture into the pan, and freeze overnight. Remove from the freezer for about 15 minutes before slicing into slabs and serving with the Mint Crème Anglaise on page 61.

HINT: This terrine can be kept in the freezer for up to a week.

Whole Earth Foods was started by Craig Sams, one of the pioneers of the organic movement, who was extolling the beliefs of macrobiotics and organic farming over thirty-five years ago, when the majority of us had not even begun to think about the effects of conventional farming methods on the environment and our health. Cocoa Crunch, a naughty yet healthy breakfast cereal adored by adults and children alike, is one of the many delicious organic foods produced by Whole Earth.

COCOA
CRUNCH

Preparation time: 10 minutes
Cooking time: 35–40 minutes
Use: large roasting pan or baking tray
Makes: 1lb, 2oz

1 1/4 cups sugar

1/2 cup water

1/4 cup vegetable oil

3 ounces milk chocolate,
preferably 34% cocoa content, chopped

2 teaspoons honey

3 heaped cups old-fashioned oats

4 1/2 cups Rice Krispies (or puffed rice cereal)

1/2 cup dried shredded coconut

1/3 cup cocoa powder

Preheat the oven to 350°F.

Line a large baking tray with parchment paper. Alternatively, butter the pan and dust with flour to coat, shaking out any excess.

Melt the sugar in the water over low heat to make a syrup without caramelizing it. Remember not to stir or disturb the sugar and water mixture at all while it is melting. Let the syrup cool until warm and then add the vegetable oil and chocolate, and let it melt in the syrup. Add the honey to the syrup and mix well.

In a large bowl, mix together the oats, Rice Krispies, coconut, and cocoa. Add the syrup mixture to the dry ingredients and mix thoroughly. Spread the mixture onto the prepared baking tray to a thickness of about a half-inch.

Bake for about 35 to 40 minutes, and, using a fork, turn the Cocoa Crunch regularly. Be careful not to crush it into fine crumbs though; it should remain as chunks, like a granola.

It is better to undercook the Cocoa Crunch as it will burn easily, especially around the sides of the baking tray, so do watch it.

HINT: Dip the spoon you are going to use to measure the honey into some oil first, to prevent the honey from sticking to the spoon.

This crumbly cookie from Brittany is traditionally a plain cookie which has so much butter in it that any other flavor seems superfluous. When working on some cookie ideas we couldn't resist trying to rival the traditional English chocolate-coated digestive cookie with this ultra indulgent one, coated in our milk and dark chocolate.

BRETON

BUTTER COOKIES

Preparation time: 10 minutes
Chilling time: 15 minutes
Cooking time: 15–20 minutes
Use: 2$^1/_2$-inch fluted cookie cutter
Makes: 50

2$^3/_4$ cups all-purpose flour

large pinch of salt

$^2/_3$ cup sugar

$^3/_4$ cup plus 2 tablespoons (1$^3/_4$ sticks) unsalted butter, chilled and diced

1 large egg, lightly beaten

$^1/_2$ teaspoon vanilla extract

two 3$^1/_2$-oz. bars milk chocolate or 2 ounces each of milk, dark, Maya Gold (or good-quality, dark, orange-flavored chocolate), and white chocolate, broken into pieces for dipping

Preheat the oven to 325°F. Butter a large baking sheet.

Sift together the flour and the salt. Add the sugar and butter and blend in a food processor or else rub between your fingertips until the mixture resembles bread crumbs. Add the egg and the vanilla and blend again or mix together with your hands, until the mixture comes together as a firm dough. Wrap in plastic wrap and chill for at least 15 minutes.

Roll out on a lightly floured board to a thickness of about an eighth-inch. Cut out the cookies using the fluted cutter.

Place on the baking sheet and bake for 15 to 20 minutes or until light golden brown. Cool on a wire rack.

Once the cookies have cooled, melt the chocolate in the top of a double boiler over barely simmering water. If using one flavor of chocolate only, select a bowl that you can fit your hand into so you can dip the cookies into it. If using white chocolate, be very careful when melting it and make sure that the bowl does not touch the water as the chocolate will seize easily. If you are using a variety of flavors of chocolate, once you've melted each one, pour the individual chocolates onto separate small plates and dip the surface of each cookie in the chocolate before returning them to the wire rack to set.

The cookies can simply have one surface dipped in the chocolate or you could decorate by drizzling white chocolate over a cookie previously dipped in dark or milk chocolate. You can also dip only half the cookie with chocolate if you prefer.

HINT: The most effective way of melting chocolate is to microwave it very slowly on medium in short bursts. To melt a third-cup chocolate pieces, microwave for 30 seconds, then continue in 10-second bursts, stirring in between each one.

Jo Gilks finds there are times when she can't wait to tuck into a meaty stew with someone, as so many of her friends seem to have become vegans or vegetarians or developed food allergies. This cake is part of the repertoire that enables her to feed them. Made with polenta, which is cornmeal rather than a flour, it satisfies all those people whose wheat-free diets prevent them from eating many of the chocolate recipes she would usually make.

POLENTA CHOCOLATE

CAKE

Preparation time: 25 minutes
Cooking time: 40 minutes
Use: 10-inch springform, deep-sided cake pan
Serves: 10

8 ounces dark chocolate,
minimum 60% cocoa content, broken into pieces

$^1/_2$ cup (1 stick) unsalted butter

5 large eggs, separated

$^2/_3$ cup sugar

1 cup fine polenta (cornmeal)

$^1/_4$ cup dark rum

confectioners' sugar for dusting

Preheat the oven to 350°F. Butter and flour the cake pan.

Melt the chocolate and the butter in the top of a double boiler over barely simmering water. Beat together the egg yolks with half of the sugar until the mixture is thick and creamy. Fold into the chocolate mixture.

In another bowl, beat the egg whites with the remaining sugar until stiff peaks form. Stir the polenta and rum into the chocolate mixture and then fold in the beaten whites. Spoon into the prepared cake pan and bake in the oven for about 40 minutes. Remove from the oven and let cake cool in the pan (it will sink as it cools). Dust with confectioners' sugar before serving.

HINT: For a crisp crust, add all the sugar to the egg yolks
and beat the egg whites without any sugar.

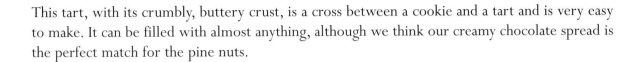

This tart, with its crumbly, buttery crust, is a cross between a cookie and a tart and is very easy to make. It can be filled with almost anything, although we think our creamy chocolate spread is the perfect match for the pine nuts.

ITALIAN PINE NUT TART
WITH CHOCOLATE SPREAD

Preparation time: 35 minutes
Chilling time: 45 minutes
Cooking time: 30–35 minutes
Use: 9-inch removable bottomed fluted tart pan
Serves: 6–8

PASTRY DOUGH

2¹/₄ cups all-purpose flour

1 teaspoon baking powder

¹/₃ cup (³/₄ stick) plus 1 tablespoon unsalted butter, cold, plus a little melted for greasing

²/₃ cup sugar

2 large eggs, beaten

about 2 tablespoons water

FILLING

11 ounces chocolate hazelnut spread (about 1¹/₂ cups)

TOPPING

1 large egg yolk

1 tablespoon milk

3 tablespoons pine nuts

1 tablespoon confectioners' sugar for dusting

Preheat the oven to 350°F. Lightly brush the inside of the tart pan with a little melted butter.

To make the dough, sift the flour and baking powder into a bowl and rub in the butter until the mixture resembles bread crumbs. Add the sugar and then mix in the eggs and some of the water. Mix together using your hands until it forms a ball. Add more water if necessary. Turn onto a lightly floured board and knead gently using the heel of your hand until the mixture is smooth and even. Cover and chill for 45 minutes.

Roll out three-quarters of the dough on a lightly floured board to a size larger than the tart pan. Press lightly into the prepared tart tin and trim. Spoon the chocolate spread into the pie shell to cover it. Roll out the remaining dough and place it on top of the chocolate spread. Press the edges of the top and bottom crusts together to seal them.

To make the topping, beat together the egg yolk and milk, then brush it over the top crust. Sprinkle the pine nuts evenly on top of that and bake for 30 to 35 minutes until light brown. Dust with confectioners' sugar and let cool before serving.

HINT: Pine nuts burn very quickly so keep an eye on this tart during the later stages of baking.

ABRACADABRA

These heavenly brownies are quick, easy, and totally indulgent. They are perfect with coffee or equally delicious served with crème fraîche or ice cream as dessert. Make sure you use the correct size baking or roasting pan and take care not to overcook them. As a rule, when you start to smell them, they are usually close to being done: you are better off removing them too soon and putting them back, which does them no harm at all!

CHOCOLATE AND CHERRY
BROWNIES

Preparation time: 15 minutes
Cooking time: 25 minutes
Makes: 28 brownies
Use: 13 x 10-inch pan, at least 2 inches deep

1$^1/_3$ cups (2$^3/_4$ sticks) unsalted butter

three 3$^1/_2$-oz. bars dark chocolate,
minimum 60% cocoa content, broken into pieces

5 large eggs

2$^1/_3$ cups granulated sugar

1 tablespoon vanilla extract

1$^1/_2$ cups all-purpose flour

1 teaspoon salt

9 ounces dried cherries (about 1$^1/_2$ cups)

Preheat the oven to 350°F. Line the baking pan with parchment paper or else grease the pan with butter.

Melt the butter and chocolate together in the top of a double boiler over barely simmering water. In a large bowl, beat the eggs, sugar, and vanilla extract together until the mixture is thick and creamy and coats the back of a spoon. Once the butter and the chocolate have melted, remove from the heat and beat into the egg mixture. Sift the flour and salt together, then add them to the batter, and continue to beat until smooth. Stir in the dried cherries.

Pour into the roasting pan, ensuring the mixture is evenly distributed in the pan. Bake in the oven for 20 to 25 minutes or until the whole of the top has formed a light brown crust that has started to crack. This giant brownie should not wobble, but should remain gooey on the inside.

Let cool for about 20 minutes before cutting into large squares while still in the pan. The parchment paper, is using, should peel off easily.

HINT: Try adding nuts or other dried fruits as an alternative to the cherries, or make plain chocolate brownies without any extras at all.

This cake is incredibly quick and easy to make and the ground-up cinnamon stick topping reminds us of why we should always freshly grind our spices. Melody Talbot has lived in New York, London, Sydney, and Verbier and has always moved to her family's next destination with a batch of her favorite recipes. This one was scribbled on a scrap of paper at a gathering of mothers from her children's school in New York.

CHOCOLATE CHIP CAKE
WITH CINNAMON STICK TOPPING

Preparation time: 15 minutes
Cooking time: 50–60 minutes
Use: 9-inch springform cake pan
Serves: 8

TOPPING

2 cinnamon sticks or 1 teaspoon ground cinnamon

$1/3$ cup ($3/4$ stick) unsalted butter

$1/4$ cup granulated sugar

CAKE

$1/2$ cup (1 stick) unsalted butter, softened

1 cup granulated sugar

2 large eggs

$1^1/4$ cups sour cream or whole milk yogurt

1 teaspoon vanilla extract

$3^1/3$ cups self-rising flour
(or all-purpose flour with 4 teaspoons baking powder and one teaspoon salt added)

two $3^1/2$-oz. bars dark chocolate, minimum 60% cocoa content, chopped

Preheat the oven to 350°F. Butter and flour the cake pan.

To make the topping, grind the cinnamon sticks in a mortar and pestle until you have quite a fine powder with a few threads of the cinnamon stick remaining, as these give an added intensity of flavor.

Melt the butter and add the sugar and the cinnamon, stirring well. Set aside.

To make the cake, cream the butter and sugar, add the eggs, and continue to beat until smooth. Add the sour cream or yogurt, and the vanilla extract, and mix well. Sift in the flour and add the chocolate. Stir.

Pour the batter into the cake pan, then evenly spread the topping over the batter using the back of a spoon.

Bake in the oven for 50 to 60 minutes. Let cool in the pan before turning out.

HINT: Try to find cinnamon from Sri Lanka or the Seychelles. Avoid cassia, which is often passed off as cinnamon, but has a much cruder flavor and a tougher bark.

OLD TIMERS

The rain forest has existed for at least 40 million years and although it now covers just two percent of the earth's surf
40 percent of all species of animals and plants live there. By 1990, half of the world's rain forests had been
destroyed and they are still being felled at an alarming rate of about 142,000 square kilometers per year.

This wonderfully simple Kuglòf recipe was given to Csilla Fodor by her Hungarian grandmother, Eszter, who still lives in Oroshàza in south-eastern Hungary. Csilla has fond memories of spending summer holidays with her as a child when this cake, speckled with chocolate, was a great luxury after the bland food of her strict boarding school.

HUNGARIAN
KUGLÒF

Preparation time: 30 minutes
Cooking time: 55 minutes
Use: 8-inch kugelhof ring mold
Serves: 8

6 large eggs, separated

1³/₄ cups sugar

³/₄ cup plus 2 tablespoons (1³/₄ sticks) unsalted butter, softened

3¹/₃ cups flour

1 cup milk

1 teaspoon lemon juice

one 3¹/₂-oz. bar dark chocolate, minimum 60% cocoa content, grated

confectioners' sugar for dusting

Preheat the oven to 275°F.

Brush the inside of the ring mold thoroughly with a little melted butter. Dust with flour.

Beat together the eggs yolks, sugar, and the butter. Sift the flour and add it to the batter, along with the milk and lemon juice, and mix well. In a large bowl, beat the egg whites until soft peaks form, then fold them gently into the batter. Divide the batter in half and add the grated chocolate to one of the halves.

Spoon the plain batter into the bottom of the ring mold, then top with the chocolate batter. Bake for about 55 minutes or until the kuglof cracks slightly on the top.

Remove from the oven and let cool for about 10 minutes before turning out onto a wire rack. Once the kuglof is completely cooled, dust with confectioners' sugar before serving.

HINT: To ensure the cake does not stick to the pan, place the ring mold in the freezer for 30 minutes before brushing it with butter and then dusting with flour.

Claire Fry is the graphic designer who has worked on both the Green & Black's and New Covent Garden Soup Company brands. She loves baking cakes and often makes elaborate themed ones for close friends. Her "Bandstand on Clapham Common" and "The Royal Albert Hall" were both wedding cakes for couples who enjoyed walking their dogs and singing in a choir. This recipe is the one she claims is infallible and lends itself to different shapes. It is delicious filled with apricot jam and covered with caramel bar or fudge sauce.

DEVIL'S
FOOD CAKE

Preparation time: 15 minutes
Cooking time: 30–35 minutes
Use: two eight-inch round cake pans with deep sides
Makes: 10–12 large slices

2^1/$_2$ cups all-purpose flour

^{1}/$_2$ teaspoon baking powder

2 teaspoons baking soda

large pinch of salt

1 cup cocoa powder

2 cups cold water

1 cup margarine or shortening

2^1/$_2$ cups sugar

4 large eggs

7 ounces apricot jam (about ^{3}/$_4$ cup)

Caramel Bar or Fudge Sauce, see page 61

Preheat the oven to 350°F.

Sift the flour with the baking powder, baking soda, and salt. Blend the cocoa with the water and set aside. Cream the margarine or shortening with a wooden spoon and add the sugar. Cream until light and very soft.

Beat the eggs until frothy, add to the creamed mixture a little at a time and beat well. Stir in the flour alternately with the blended cocoa and water. Divide the mixture between the two pans and bake for 30 to 35 minutes or until a skewer inserted into the center comes out clean. Let cool for a few minutes in the pan, then turn out onto a wire rack. Let cool completely before filling with apricot jam or a filling of your choice. Pour Caramel Bar Sauce or Fudge Sauce over the top and down the sides of the cake.

HINT: Don't be tempted to use butter when making this cake as it is definitely lighter and has a better texture made with margarine.

OLD TIMERS

Treat your friends to three different *pôts de crème*. They are exceedingly rich so why not serve them in egg cups on a dessert plate with a little coffee spoon and delicate Chocolate Tuiles (see page 106) or plain butter cookies?

THREE PÔTS
DE CRÈME

Preparation time: 30 minutes
Chilling time: 2–3 hours
Use: egg cups or other small unusual containers – try liqueur glasses
Serves: 6

1³/₄ cups light cream

1 vanilla bean

1 ounce dark chocolate,
minimum 60% cocoa content, broken into pieces

1 ounce Maya Gold Chocolate, or
other good-quality, dark, orange-flavored
chocolate, broken into pieces

2 ounces white chocolate, broken into pieces

6 large egg yolks

¹/₄ cup sugar

¹/₂ teaspoon salt

Gently heat the cream with the vanilla bean until bubbles begin to form at the edge, but make sure the cream does not boil. Remove from the heat and set aside to infuse.

Melt the chocolates separately in heatproof bowls sitting over saucepans of barely simmering water. (Keep the saucepans of water as you will need them later on.) Remove the bowls from the heat and let the chocolates cool, then beat two of the egg yolks into each of the melted chocolates until the mixtures are smooth. Combine the sugar and salt, and stir one-third of the mixture into each chocolate mixture until completely dissolved.

Remove the vanilla bean from the cream and gently stir one-third of the cream into each chocolate mixture until well blended. Replace the bowls over the saucepans of simmering water.

Cook until each mixture coats the back of a spoon, stirring all the time.

Pour each chocolate mixture into your chosen containers and chill for about two to three hours or until the mixture has set.

HINT: Melt the chocolate before adding it to the cream. If you try to add chopped or grated chocolate to the hot mixture, it will seize and your pôts will be grainy.

"Celebrations," a box of assorted miniature chocolate candies, was the inspiration for this intriguing brownie recipe sent in by Jane Holden. As Jane says, it "will keep your visitors guessing" as each brownie contains a different chocolate candy, with a very different texture and flavor from the next one.

CELEBRATION
BROWNIES

Preparation time: 20 minutes
Cooking time: 25–30 minutes
Use: 11 x 7-inch baking pan
Makes: 15

$^3/_4$ cup plus 2 tablespoons (1$^3/_4$ sticks) unsalted butter

one 3$^1/_2$-oz. bar dark chocolate, minimum 60% cocoa content, broken into pieces

1$^2/_3$ cups soft dark brown sugar

4 large eggs

1 teaspoon vanilla extract

1$^1/_2$ cups self-rising flour
(or all-purpose flour with 2$^1/_4$ teaspoons baking powder and $^3/_4$ teaspoon salt added)

pinch of salt

one 10$^1/_4$-oz. box of "Celebrations"
or mixture of other miniature candy bars of your choice, such as Peanut Butter Cups, Mr. Goodbar, Butterfingers, 5th Avenue, Peppermint Patties, etc.

Preheat the oven to 350°F.

Brush the pan with melted butter, then line it with parchment paper, if you like.

Melt the butter and the chocolate in the top of a double boiler over barely simmering water. Remove from the heat and add the sugar.

Beat the eggs and the vanilla and add to the chocolate batter. Sift the flour and stir it into the batter, along with the salt (and baking powder, if using all-purpose flour).

Unwrap the miniature chocolate candies. Pour half the batter into the tin and then carefully place the chocolates so that there will be at least one in each portion when it's cut. Pour in the remaining batter, ensuring that the candies are covered.

Bake for about 25 to 30 minutes, until the top is crispy and the inside soft.

Let cool in the pan before cutting.

HINT: This recipe also works well with malted milk balls dotted all around the tray and then covered with the cake mixture, or try a layer of mint chocolate thins.

This recipe will find a home for those sad, brown bananas that nobody wants to eat. An old favorite, it is the perfect coffee break treat and goes well with tea or coffee.

WHITE CHOCOLATE,
WALNUT, AND BANANA LOAF

Preparation time: 30 minutes
Baking time: 1–1$^{1}/_{4}$ hours
Use: 2-pound loaf pan
Makes: 1 large loaf

$^{1}/_{2}$ cup (1 stick) unsalted butter, melted

1$^{1}/_{4}$ cups all-purpose flour

2 teaspoons baking powder

$^{1}/_{2}$ teaspoon baking soda

$^{1}/_{2}$ teaspoon salt

$^{2}/_{3}$ cup sugar

2 large eggs

4 small, very ripe bananas, mashed

one 3$^{1}/_{2}$-oz. bar good-quality white chocolate, chopped into large chunks

$^{1}/_{2}$ cup walnuts, chopped

1 teaspoon vanilla extract

Preheat oven to 350°F. Brush the inside of the loaf pan with a little melted butter, then dust with flour.

Mix the flour, baking powder, baking soda, and salt in a bowl. In a separate bowl whisk the melted butter and sugar together. Beat in the eggs, one at a time, then whisk in the mashed bananas. Add the white chocolate, walnuts, and vanilla. Add the dry ingredients to the banana batter in three stages, stirring after each addition.

Pour into the loaf pan and bake for one to one and a quarter hours.

Slide a spatula around the edge of the loaf and leave it in the pan to cool.

HINT: Nigella's Blond Icing (see page 181) is delicious poured over this cake.

OLD TIMERS

You only have to spend a short time in the rain forest to understand why growing cacao organically makes sense. The cacao trees are planted under indigenous trees for shade, are sheltered from the wind and sun, and don't dry out when it gets too hot. Any insect pests that eat the crop are picked off by natural predators.

The forest floor is a carpet of leaf litter which fills the soil with the nutrients that help the plants to grow without any need of chemical fertilizers. This results in a bio-diverse environment where cacao trees thrive among forest flora and fauna.

Slashing and burning rain forest trees to intensify the cultivation of crops has destroyed large tracts of the rain forest. The natural pest predators cannot live without trees, and so many of the conventional growers use chemical insect-killers and if these insect-killers are not used carefully, they can poison other wildlife or wipe out their food chains. Less leaf litter means the soil runs out of nutrients, so artificial fertilizers have to be used. If too much is used, the excess can run off into streams and rivers and pollute them, which harms the animals that live in and depend on the river water.

Konditor & Cook is the place we go to each day for our lunch. We try to resist as it is a bit of a luxury, but those beautiful, minimalist, pale blue bags keep appearing at lunchtime. Now and again eyeing up the pastries proves to be too much and one of us, unable to resist the temptation, buys one. This recipe for Chocolate Biscuit Cake was kindly given to us by chef Gerhard Jenne. We promised him we would never try to make it on a bigger scale!

KONDITOR & COOK

CHOCOLATE COOKIE CAKE

Preparation time: 15 minutes
Chilling time: 4 hours
Use: 8 x 3-inch loaf pan
Makes: 10 large, very rich slices

$^1/_2$ cup (1 stick) plus 1 tablespoon unsalted butter

$^1/_4$ cup golden syrup (if unavailable, use corn syrup)

two 3$^1/_2$-oz. bars dark chocolate,
minimum 60% cocoa content, broken into pieces

1 egg

4 digestive biscuits (cookies)
or 2 ounces graham crackers (about 8)

$^1/_2$ cup whole walnuts

$^1/_4$ cup golden raisins

$^1/_3$ cup candied cherries, reserving a few
for decoration

Line the loaf pan with parchment paper or alternativly butter the pan. Set aside.

Melt the butter and syrup together in a small saucepan over gentle heat until they begin to boil.

Melt the chocolate in the top of a double boiler over barely simmering water, then mix thoroughly with the butter and golden syrup.

Pasteurize the egg by beating it slowly and continuously into the hot chocolate mixture.

Into another bowl, break up the cookies or graham crackers into large chunks; remember, they will be broken further when mixed, so don't make them too small.

Add the walnuts, raisins and most of the cherries to the broken cookies.

Pour the chocolate mixture on to the cookie mixture and mix together with a spatula or wooden spoon.

Press the mixture into the pan and decorate with the reserved cherries. Let set in the fridge for about four hours. Remove from the fridge, peel off the paper, and cut into slices or cubes. Serve chilled.

HINT: To make this recipe more appealing to children,
why not replace 100g of dark chocolate with milk chocolate?

DARK
ICING

Ideal for covering a sophisticated chocolate cake

one 3¹/₂-oz. bar dark chocolate,
minimum 60% cocoa content, chopped

¹/₄ cup (¹/₂ stick) unsalted butter, cubed

Melt the chocolate in the top of a double boiler over barely simmering water. Remove from the heat, add the butter, and stir until the butter has melted and the sauce has the consistency of thick pouring cream.

Use the back of a teaspoon to spread the icing over the top and sides of the cake. Let it set. If refrigerated, the icing will lose its sheen.

CHOCOLATE
GLAZE

A traditional, sweet chocolate glaze

one 3¹/₂-oz. bar dark chocolate,
minimum 60% cocoa content, chopped

²/₃ cup confectioners' sugar

3 tablespoons unsalted butter, cubed

3 tablespoons water

Melt the chocolate in the top of a double boiler over barely simmering water. Leaving the top pan over the hot water, sift the confectioners' sugar and add it to the melted chocolate, stir well, then add the butter and stir until fully incorporated. Remove the top pan from the heat and add the water, one tablespoon at a time. Use the glaze while it is still warm – it will run if it is too hot and it will not spread if it is too cold.

DUSKY BUTTER
FROSTING

Ideal for filling and covering a children's cake.

one 3¹/₂-oz. bar milk chocolate

³/₄ cup (1¹/₂ sticks) unsalted butter, softened

1¹/₂ cups confectioners' sugar

Melt the chocolate in the top of a double boiler over barely simmering water. Set aside to cool until tepid. Cream the butter until softened, add the sugar, and cream together well. Add the chocolate to the mixture and beat together well.

ORANGE

DUST

A more unusual topping

4 oranges

1¹/₂ cups granulated sugar

¹/₂ cup water

oil for greasing

Scrub the oranges and pat them dry. Using a vegetable peeler, remove the top layer of peel, but ensure you don't remove the white pith. Bring the sugar and the water to a boil and, without stirring, boil for about 10 minutes or until it begins to form a syrup (test by dropping some onto a plate; if it begins to set immediately, it is ready). Add the orange peel and continue to boil without stirring for another 10 minutes. Brush some oil onto a baking sheet and, using a pair of tongs, transfer the caramelized peel to the baking sheet. Let cool and dry completely before pulverising in a food processor. Store in an airtight container for sprinkling over cakes and puddings.

CHOCOLATE

GANACHE

A thick, rich, and creamy filling or topping. If you need more,
simply increase the quantities, keeping the ingredients in the same proportions.

10 ounces dark chocolate,
minimum 60% cocoa content, chopped

1¹/₄ cups heavy cream

Put the chocolate into a large bowl. Heat the cream until it begins to simmer, pour it over the chocolate, and immediately begin to whisk. Continue to whisk until the mixture has cooled and thickened.

NIGELLA'S BLOND

ICING

two 3¹/₂-oz. bars white chocolate

¹/₄ cup (¹/₂ stick) unsalted butter

1 cup crème fraîche or sour cream

³/₄ cup confectioners' sugar, sifted

Melt the chocolate and the butter in the top of a double boiler over barely simmering water. Remove and let cool a little, add the crème fraîche, and then gradually beat in the confectioners' sugar. Put the icing in the fridge for a little while so that it sets before you need to use it.

DRINKS TO ACCOMPANY

CHOCOLATE

Micah Carr-Hill is our Product Development Manager and also a serious lover of food. He became interested in wine when he worked in the British wine shop, Oddbins, and eight years later, has poured most of his earnings into buying wine and cooking meals for his friends and his partner, Nat, which can take days to prepare.

Micah believes there should be no rules about what you should and shouldn't drink with particular foods, but says that "chocolate and chocolate desserts are particularly difficult to match as they coat your mouth, are usually quite sweet, and chocolate itself has a certain amount of acidity." He therefore suggests a few tips:

"The one thing to bear in mind when matching wine to desserts is that it is best to choose a wine that is as sweet, if not sweeter, than the food, otherwise the wine is likely to be overpowered by what you are eating and seem unpleasantly sharp.

"However, chocolate does not always go well with traditional sweet wines such as Sauternes, and as chocolate is often married with cherries, raisins, dates, and other such fruits, it often makes sense to match them with drinks that have similar flavors. For example, a chocolate dessert with raspberry would go well with a raspberry liqueur like Framboise or raspberry beer from Belgium.

"Lighter desserts made with white and milk chocolate work well with a fresh, spritzy, grapey Moscato d'Asti or a slightly heavier Orange Muscat (especially if they contain orange). Belgian cherry or raspberry beers would also be good.

"Desserts made with a dark chocolate demand a richer and fuller wine such as a Black Muscat or a sweet Italian Recioto, made from partially dried red wine grapes. You could also try a vin doux naturels, which is a type of French wine that is made from partially fermented wine and local brandy, such as Rivesaltes, Banyuls, or Maury. A port, Ruby or Tawny, an Australian Liqueur Muscat, or even one of the sweeter Madeiras (Malmsey or Bual) would also be good choices.

"If you're serving a savory dish such as a mole, you need a weighty red wine to cope with the range of rich flavors kicking about. A big Syrah, Shiraz, or Zinfandel would cope as would a big Italian red such as an Amarone or Barolo.

"Stouts, porters, and dark beers made from chocolate malts (that have been highly roasted) are also good companions as is black coffee, irrespective of whether there is coffee in the recipe or not.

"The following are my suggestions, but remember that there are no hard and fast rules:

COMPLEMENTARY FLAVORS

APRICOT – light, sweet Muscat or a Hungarian Tokaji

APPLES – sweet Oloroso Sherry or a Liqueur Muscat

BANANA – Australian Liqueur Muscat, Tokaji, sweet Madeira, or Tawny Port

BROWNIES – Black coffee or a good Scotch

COFFEE – Coffee, Orange Muscat, Australian Liqueur Muscat, or a sweet Oloroso sherry such as Matusalem

COOKIES – Tea, coffee, milk

DATES – Liqueur Muscat or sweet Oloroso sherry

FIGS – Black Muscat or sweet Oloroso sherry

GINGER – Ginger beer or ginger ale, sweet Oloroso sherry, or a Liqueur Muscat

GORGONZOLA – Sweet red Italian Recioto, late-bottled vintage Port, or Tawny Port

HARE – a big Syrah, Shiraz, or Zinfandel

HAZELNUTS – a Malmsey or Bual Madeira, or a stout made from chocolate malt

ICE CREAM – a Liqueur Muscat, sweet Oloroso or even a Pedro Ximinez (PX) sherry, a Malmsey, or Bual Madeira

LAMB – a big red from the Rhone Valley, Portugal, or southern Italy

LEMON – a very sweet late-harvest Riesling such as a Trockenbeerenauslese

MEXICAN – Chilean or Argentinian red wine, Mexican beer, or a cocktail such as a Margarita or Bloody Mary

PANNA COTTA – Recioto di Soave from Italy or an Orange Muscat

PEARS – Orange Muscat

PECAN PIE – Liqueur Muscat, sweet Oloroso Muscat, or a Malmsey or Bual Madeira

SAUSAGES – robust Spanish or Portuguese reds or a Zinfandel

STOUT CAKE – stout

TRUFFLES – eau de vie of your choice

VANILLA – late-harvest Riesling

VENISON – big Italian red such as a Barolo or something from the south of Italy such as a Salice Salentino

WALNUTS – Australian Liqueur Muscat or a sweet Oloroso sherry

WHITE CHOCOLATE – sweet white Bordeaux such as Sauternes or Barsac, or a late-harvest Riesling such as an Auslese or Beerenauslese".

Lubaantun was the center of the Maya civilization in southern Belize. A great ceremonial focus, it existed over 1,000 years ago, hidden deep in the rain forest.

In this vibrant society, the universal measure of value was the cocoa bean. As Lubaantun was situated in the Maya mountains, where cacao trees thrived in the wild, it rapidly became the economic center of the Maya world, with the cocoa bean at the heart of the economy.

In the 1850s, it was taken over by colonists, who cut down trees and established plantations. But they struggled to control nature and place names like "Go To Hell Creek" and "Hellgate" are all that remains of those desperate times.

The Maya returned to their villages in the mountains and lived by subsistence farming, trading their surplus cocoa beans for cash and growing indigenous crops using traditional methods. But in the early 1990s the price of cocoa, which had been falling for years, dropped dramatically just before harvest time as too much cocoa flooded world markets and many farmers were left unable to afford even to harvest their crops.

It was at this time that Jo Fairley and Craig Sams, who were on vacation in Belize and looking for organic cocoa beans, heard about their plight. They began to buy organic beans from the Maya, which in turn, led to their involvement with the Fairtrade foundation. Their relationship with the Toledo Cocoa Growers Association resulted in the creation of Green & Black's

Maya Gold Chocolate, sold in the UK, and the first-ever product to carry the Fairtrade Mark.

Over 300 families benefit from the sale of cocoa beans and many of the farmers have plantations with trees that are over 100 years old. They live on the land that their ancestors have farmed for thousands of years and will preserve that land for future generations.

OLD TIMERS

Saul Garcia is a Fairtrade farmer who has been farming cacao in Belize for thirty-eight years. If you visit his fifteen-acre farm set on the banks of the Columbia River, you can see more than fifteen different varieties of cacao tree, surrounded by a cascade of beautiful colors from the shrubs and crops that he plants between his cacao trees.

The bio-diversity created by planting so many different species of cacao and other plants helps to reduce the threat of bugs that cause serious damage to organically grown cacao.

Papaya, bananas, coffee, breebee, coconut, mango, breadfruit, cacao, mamey sapote, lime, *Theobroma bicolor*, avocado, cohune palm, soursop, plantain, samwood, jippy japa, golden plum, leucaena, glyricidia, craboo, orange, starfruit, vanilla, ginger, sugar cane, sorrel, and bamboo are just some of the plants Saul Garcia grows. Some are used for food or as fiber, particularly for basket weaving, others are good for the soil and there are also ornamental plants for attracting pollinators.

INDEX